Jacques Bénigne Bossuet

Devotion to the Blessed Virgin

Being the substance of all the sermons for Mary's feasts throughout the year

Jacques Bénigne Bossuet

Devotion to the Blessed Virgin

Being the substance of all the sermons for Mary's feasts throughout the year

ISBN/EAN: 9783337084943

Printed in Europe, USA, Canada, Australia, Japan

Cover: Foto ©ninafisch / pixelio.de

More available books at **www.hansebooks.com**

BOSSUET

ON

DEVOTION TO THE BLESSED VIRGIN

DEVOTION
TO THE BLESSED VIRGIN

BEING THE SUBSTANCE OF ALL THE SERMONS FOR
MARY'S FEASTS THROUGHOUT THE YEAR

BY

JACQUES BENIGNE BOSSUET

BISHOP OF MEAUX

CONDENSED, ARRANGED, AND TRANSLATED BY

F. M. CAPES

WITH AN INTRODUCTION BY

THE REV. WILLIAM T. GORDON

PRIEST OF THE LONDON ORATORY

LONGMANS, GREEN, AND CO.

39 PATERNOSTER ROW, LONDON

NEW YORK AND BOMBAY

1899

Nihil Obstat.:

> GULIELMUS T. GORDON,
> *Congr. Orat.; Censor Deputatus.*

Imprimatur:

> HERBERTUS CARDINALIS VAUGHAN,
> *Archiepiscopus Westmonast.*

Die 22 Januarii, 1899.

TO

THE NINE CHOIRS OF ANGELS

THIS ENGLISH FORM

OF A GREAT PREACHER'S THOUGHTS ABOUT THEIR QUEEN

is Dedicated.

"*Regina Angelorum, ora pro nobis!*"

INTRODUCTION.

BOSSUET's Sermons on the Feasts of our Blessed Lady number about twenty—there being in many cases two or three, and sometimes even four, for the same festival. Some of these are mere repetitions of each other as to matter, with slight changes in form to suit different audiences or occasions, whilst others, though not actually verbal repetitions, are so much alike in portions that, presented to readers in their integrity, they would be simply wearisome. The writer of this English version has not therefore attempted a literal or consecutive translation of the sermons as they stand, but has aimed at so selecting, combining, and condensing them, as to produce a set of discourses on Mary's Feasts throughout the year that should contain the whole substance of Bossuet's teaching ; and in passages of a strictly theo logical nature the actual words of the preacher have been adhered to as closely as they could be in English.

Repetitions have been, as a rule, avoided, and where this could not well be done, the translator has tried to account for the repeated matter by reference to what has gone before, so as to show its necessity. On the other hand, care has been taken not to omit anything of importance to the preacher's train of thought; and it is hoped that this small volume fairly sets forth the substantial contents of Bossuet's twenty sermons on the Feasts of our Blessed Lady.

It may seem to many that another book on Devotion to our Blessed Lady is not needed as so many already exist. But different books suit different minds, and I have long wished to be able to put into the hands of English readers Bossuet's learned, logical, and at the same time devout exposition of Catholic doctrine on our Lady's dignity, and on the relations which Almighty God has willed to establish between her and the members of the Mystical Body of her Divine Son. Bossuet's great ability and profound learning must command respect, and his readers cannot fail to be impressed with the authority with which his familiarity with the Holy Scriptures, and his wide knowledge of the writings of the early Fathers of the Church, enable him to speak.

Catholics, as well as non-Catholics, may need to have brought home to them that devotion to Mary is not merely a beautiful addition to Christian piety, but that it is essential to the full comprehension of the mystery of the Incarnation, as is shown by the action of the Council of Ephesus which not only decreed that the title of "Mother of God" was rightly given to Mary but condemned as heretics those who denied it.

Now the very foundation of Bossuet's teaching on the honour and love due to our Blessed Lady, is that her co-operation in the Incarnation formed an integral part of the merciful design of God for the redemption of man, and that "our love of our Divine Saviour is the unchangeable foundation of our devotion to the Blessed Virgin". In proof of these propositions Bossuet brings out so wonderfully the hidden meaning of the sacred words of Scripture, and supports his interpretation with so many quotations from the writings of the Fathers, that we are filled with admiration, and the hearts of simple Christians are delighted to find how their instinctive love of Mary, and confidence in the power of her intercession, are in harmony with the dogmatic teaching of the Saints and Doctors of the Church in all ages.

To non-Catholics Bossuet's explanation of the doctrine of the Immaculate Conception will be most useful—that doctrine has been so persistently misunderstood, and often so persistently misrepresented, that Bossuet's clear and logical defence of it will be invaluable, and will impress them the more from the fact that it was written so long before the Vatican Council defined it as an article of faith.

From Bossuet's teaching we learn that, to quote Cardinal Manning's words, "the titles of honour given to Mary are not metaphors but truths—they express, not poetical or rhetorical ideas, but true and living relations between her and her Divine Son and between her and ourselves".

I will conclude by again quoting Cardinal Manning, who warns Catholics "never to shrink from calling her that which God has made her; never to fear to seek her in those offices of grace with which God has invested her". "May our Divine Lord," he continues, "preserve us from giving way a hair's breadth, before the face of anti-Catholic censors, in the filial piety of our faith, or the childlike confidence of our devotion towards His Blessed Mother and our own."

WILLIAM T. GORDON,
Of the Oratory.

TABLE OF CONTENTS.

CHAPTER PAGE

I. ON THE GROUNDS OF DEVOTION TO THE BLESSED VIRGIN AND THE SAINTS (Preached on a Feast of Mary's Conception) 1

II. THE BLESSED VIRGIN'S CONCEPTION 17

III. MARY A FORESHADOWING OF CHRIST (Preached on a Feast of her Nativity) 39

IV. THE BLESSED VIRGIN'S NATIVITY 52

V. THE FEAST OF THE ANNUNCIATION 69

VI. THE FEAST OF THE VISITATION 83

VII. THE HIDDENNESS AND POVERTY OF JESUS AND MARY (Preached on a Feast of the Purification) . . 99

VIII. THE BLESSED VIRGIN'S COMPASSION 111

IX. THE ASSUMPTION OF MARY 132

I.

ON THE GROUNDS OF DEVOTION TO THE BLESSED VIRGIN AND THE SAINTS, AND ON THE NATURE OF TRUE DEVOTION.

(From a Sermon preached on a Feast of Mary's Conception.)

DEVOTION to the Blessed Virgin is a matter concerning which there are two important points to be specially considered:—first, the *grounds* on which this devotion is solidly founded; secondly, the *rules* to be invariably followed in practising it. A clear understanding of these points will help us to honour her as true Christians ought, not on one of her feasts only, but on all those presented in succession by the Church to the observance of the Faithful.

With Advent, which opens the ecclesiastical year, comes the Feast of Our Lady's Conception. As on this day we really commemorate the first moment of her existence, and consequently that of our first relations with her as our most favoured fellow-creature, there could not be a more fitting day for treating the subject of *why*, and *how*, we are to pay her homage.

I.

First, then, on what basis is our devotion to Mary founded? "No one," says the Apostle, "can lay any foundation but the one that has been laid—that is, Jesus Christ." Now, in a pre-eminent manner, Our Divine Saviour is the foundation of the honour we pay to the Blessed Virgin; because we have *received Him*, in fact, *through her*. God predestined Mary, before all time, to be the means of giving Jesus Christ to the world. Having called her to so glorious a ministry, He did not choose that she should be a merely passive channel of His grace. He made her, farther, a voluntary instrument who should contribute to the great work by the use of her own will. Is not this clear from the manner in which the Incarnation was announced to Mary? When the moment for accomplishing that Mystery—which has kept all nature expectant throughout the ages—has arrived, the Eternal Father sends an angel to make it known to her; and the angel awaits the maiden's decision, so that the great act shall not be performed without her consent. The moment she has given this the heavens are opened, the Son of God is made man, and the world has a Saviour.

Hence, the love and longing of Mary were in a measure necessary for our salvation. St. Thomas declares that "the fulness of grace she then received was so great that it brought her to a most intimate union with the *Author of Grace;* that this fitted her to

Devotion to the Blessed Virgin and Saints. 3

receive into her holy womb the One who *contains all graces;* and that thus, in conceiving Him, she became in some sort *the source* of that grace which He was to pour forth over all mankind—and so *concurred* in giving the human race its Deliverer".

There is a necessary consequence of this fact which is not sufficiently borne in mind: namely, that God having once elected to give us Jesus Christ through the Blessed Virgin, this order of things can never change; for the gifts of God are "without repentance". It is, and always will be, true, that having once received the Author of our salvation through her, we shall necessarily continue to receive help towards that salvation in the same manner. The Incarnate Word is the universal principle of grace; but the Christian life in its various phases consists in the *particular applications* of the grace proceeding from this principle to the individual needs of each soul. Mary, having been once chosen as the means by which grace should come into the world, has, as a natural consequence, her share in its application to the souls of men for their salvation.

Theology recognises three principal operations of Jesus Christ's grace: God *calls* us; God *justifies* us; God grants us *perseverance.* The calling is the first step; justification constitutes our progress; perseverance brings the journey to an end, and gives us in our true country what can never be had together on earth —rest and glory.

Now, every Christian knows that for all these three states the power of Christ is needed; but perhaps few really believe how clearly Scripture indicates Mary's perpetual association with their work in the soul. A few words, however, will prove this.

(1) The Divine *Call* is typified by the sudden enlightenment that St. John the Baptist received in his mother's womb. If we reflect on this miracle we see in it an image of sinners called by grace. John, hidden within his mother's flesh, is in utter blindness and deafness: but who so blind and deaf as the sinner? The thunder of God's judgments breaks over him unheard; the very light of the Gospel fails to open his eyes. Yet, in the dark places where he has hidden himself, does not God find him out, and show him the truth as in a lightning-flash? Again: Jesus comes to John unexpectedly: He *prevents* him: He suddenly rouses and attracts his hitherto insensible heart. And how does God come to the sinner? He comes unasked, unsought, and calls him to repentance; He inspires the sinful heart with a secret, unaccountable, disgust and bitterness that compel it to regret its lost peace and to long, almost unconsciously, for reconciliation. Even whilst the soul is in the act of fleeing from Him it suddenly finds itself arrested and compelled to turn.

But once more:—when God gives us, in the leaping of the unborn St. John, an image of the sinner "prevented by grace," He shows us at the same time

Devotion to the Blessed Virgin and Saints. 5

Mary's concurrence in the work. If John, thus called, as it were struggles to escape from the prison that confines him, at whose voice does he so act? "For, behold, as soon as the voice of *Thy salutation* sounded in my ears, the infant in my womb leapt for joy!" So St. Elizabeth declares; and St. Ambrose says that Mary "raised John the Baptist above nature," and by her mere voice caused him to drink in the spirit of holiness, before he had breathed the breath of life :—"he obeyed before he was brought forth". According to the same doctor, the grace given to Mary was so great that it not only kept her a virgin, but conferred the gift of innocence on those she visited. Hence we need not wonder if St. John, whom the mother of His Saviour anointed, so to speak, with the oil of her presence and the perfume of her purity for three months, was born and lived (as the Church's tradition holds) in perfect freedom from sin.

(2) *Justification*, God's next great work in man's soul, is represented at the marriage of Cana in the persons of the Apostles. For what says the Evangelist? "Jesus turned water into wine" (His first miracle); "and He showed His glory, and His disciples believed in Him." The Apostles had already been called, but they had not hitherto had a lively enough *faith* to be justified :—justification being attributed to faith as the first principle, or root, of all grace, though not sufficient by itself for salvation. The sacred text could not express "justifying faith" in clearer terms than it

does here; but neither could it put before us more plainly the Blessed Virgin's share in this marvellous work. Was not that great miracle, confirming the Apostles' faith, the effect of Mary's charity and intercession? True:—when she first asked for the grace, she seemed to be repelled. "Woman," said the Saviour, "what is there between thee and Me? My hour has not yet come" (John ii. 4). But though these words sound rough, and appear like a curt refusal, Mary did not hold herself refused. She understood her Son; and she took His rebuff as typical of that ingenious love by which He often tests the prayer of faithful souls, only to show that humility and persevering confidence may win what a first request has not obtained. Her expectation was not deceived: Jesus, who had seemed to deny her, did what she asked; and even—St. Chrysostom says—forestalled the hour He had determined on for His first miracle, to please her. Again: this miracle wrought at Mary's prayer is unlike other miracles of Christ in being worked for a really unnecessary thing. There is no special need of more wine at their wedding feast; but His mother wishes it, and that is enough. Are we to believe it an accidental coincidence that she should interpose only in this particular miracle, which is followed by a result embodying an express image of the justification of sinners? No: there can be no doubt that the Holy Spirit intended us to understand just what St. Augustine understood by

Devotion to the Blessed Virgin and Saints. 7

the mystery ; and what, therefore, has been accepted as its meaning from the first ages of Scriptural interpretation. " The glorious Virgin "—writes the great doctor—" being Mother of our Head according to the flesh, had to be Mother of all His members according to the Spirit, by co-operating through her divinity in the spiritual birth of the children of God."

Lastly, we must go on to see how she contributes not only to the *birth* of the soul but to its faithful perseverance.

(3) As the Baptist typifies the sinner called out of darkness, and the Apostles at Cana in Galilee the soul justified by faith, so does St. John the Beloved at the foot of the Cross stand for the children of grace and adoption who *persevere with Jesus to the end*. With Mary, he follows Christ even to the Cross while the other disciples take flight, clinging with constancy to the mystical tree, and generously ready to die with his Lord. Thus, he is naturally a figure of the persevering Faithful. Now—mark this—*to John*, particularly, as we know, Christ *gives His Mother* : those whom he here typifies are to be Mary's special children. Surely, then, she will make it her peculiar care to beg the grace of perseverance for every Christian soul ?

Here, then, is the promised proof:—those who know what mysterious meanings are hidden beneath the words of the sacred text recognise, in these three examples, that Mary through her intercession is Mother alike of the called, the justified, and the persevering; and that her untiring love is in fact instrumental in every operation of grace. The great point for us to remember, as the solid ground of our devotion, is that her power with Our Lord *remains the same* now that it was during His life on earth; for natural feelings are raised and perfected, not extinguished, in glory. Hence, the most Blessed Virgin need never fear a refusal: Christ's own love pleads on the side of Mary's prayers, because the very human nature that He assumed speaks to Him through her; and thus we have, for ever pleading our cause with God, that most powerful of all human advocates—a Mother at the feet of her Son.

2.

Now, having seen the real basis on which the honour paid by the Church to Our Lady rests (and woe be to those who would fain deprive Christians of her help!) let us carefully consider in what way devotion to her should be practised; for, even though furnished with a lasting foundation for our piety, we may show it by what are only vain and superstitious practices. There is a true devotion, and a false one; and the next point to treat concerns the *kind* of worship that we owe respectively to God, to the Blessed Virgin, and to all the Saints.

The fundamental rule of the honour we pay to the

Devotion to the Blessed Virgin and Saints. 9

Blessed Virgin and the Saints is this: that we must entirely refer it all to God and to our eternal salvation. If it were not referred to God it would be a purely human act, and we surely know that the Saints, being filled with God and His glory, will not accept purely human devotion. What does "religion" mean but a *binding to God?* And how could any act that was *not* religious please His holy ones? Hence, all devotion to Mary is useless and superstitious that does not lead us to the possession of God and the enjoyment of our heavenly inheritance. This is, indeed, the general rule of all true religious worship: that it *flows from*, and *returns to*, God, and is in no wise diverted from Him by being extended to His creatures.

To come to particulars in the matter: there are two special points, concerning prayer to Our Lady and the Saints, on which the Church is accused by her enemies of erroneous practice, the first of which is "idolatry". In other words, Catholics are often charged with acting almost like the heathen in so using their canonised fellow-creatures as to be guilty of *multiplying God*, by turning them into so many minor deities to whom they pay divine homage. The folly and injustice of such an accusation is very simply proved by reference to the rule just given. The *only* honour recognised by the Church as due to her Saints is an honour strictly in accordance with that rule; which rule is itself founded upon the central principle of our Faith; namely, on the *unity* and *supremacy* of God.

We Christians adore but one God; single, omnipotent, creator and dispenser of all things; in whose name we were consecrated at baptism; and in whom *alone.* we recognise absolute sovereignty, unlimited goodness, and perfect fulness of Being. We honour the Blessed Virgin and the Saints, not by a worship of necessary service, or of subjection—for, in the order of religion, we are free as regards creatures, and subject only to God—but by an honour of brotherly love and fellowship. In them, we pay homage to wonders worked "by the right hand of the Most High"; we revere the communication to them of *His* grace—the diffusion, through them, of *His* glory. In short, what we honour in them is the very fact of their dependence on that Primary Being to Whom alone our true worship relates; the sole principle of all good, and the end of all our desires, as of theirs. We must, then, entirely repudiate the fear, professed by our enemies, that the glory of God can be diminished by our conceiving high notions of Mary and the Saints. Would it not be attributing miserable weakness to the Creator to imagine Him jealous of His own gifts, and of the light He sheds on His creatures? Just as well might we expect the sun, if he had life, to be jealous of the moon, who shines merely by reflection of his own rays! No matter how highly we may honour Mary's perfections Jesus Christ could not

Devotion to the Blessed Virgin and Saints. 11

possibly envy her, seeing that He is Himself the source of every grace she possesses. Let the critics who accuse us of idolatry in our worship of the Saints remember that they condemn, with us, the Ambroses, the Augustines, the Chrysostoms, on whose doctrine and example they know our practice to be founded, and whom they themselves acknowledge as authorities.

The second accusation commonly made against us is that we make for ourselves *many mediators*, instead of relying on " the One Sole Mediator, Jesus Christ, Who saved us with His blood " ; and our motive for this error is often, further, said to be that—like certain ancient philosophers—we deem God Himself, even though made man for us, to be inaccessible *immediately* from His extreme purity. Now, if any Catholic ever allows such a notion as this to lay hold of him, and make him put the Saints, to the smallest extent, in the place of Christ, it can only be because of his most culpable ignorance or neglect of his own Church's teaching. No one is taught so plainly as we are that we were created by God for immediate intercourse with Him ; but that we lost our privilege, for time, by sin ; and that we should have lost it also for eternity if the Son had not reconciled us to the Father by taking our sins on Himself. Hence, we ask absolutely nothing except in the name of Our Saviour, as every child who has properly learnt its catechism is fully aware. All we do, in begging the Saints' prayers, is to beg the prayers of those among our own brethren who are specially dear to that Saviour Himself because of *their supreme love for Him*. We all—Protestant and Catholic alike—ask for the prayers of our *living* friends and fellow-Christians, and all believe that "the prayer of the just man availeth much". The doctrine of "the Communion of Saints," as Catholics put it into practice, is merely the carrying out of this principle with regard to those who are already in the company of God, but whom we believe to be, through His power, still present in spirit among us, and to have our interests at heart though no longer with us in the flesh.

There is yet another principle involved in the true doctrine of honour to the Saints, which must be touched upon before we leave the subject; and that is the great advantage to ourselves contained in practising devotion towards them of a right sort. The Christian is bound to imitate what he honours, and the object of his worship must also be the model of his life. His God is a *perfect* God; and hence he must try to make himself perfect, and worship only those who have given honour to their Maker by imitating His perfections. When we venerate the Saints it is not to increase *their* glory: that is full; they have their perfect measure of it with God in heaven. We pay them homage—over and above the motive of giving glory to God—that we may incite ourselves to follow them, and we ask their prayers for the same purpose. This is the sense of the Church

Devotion to the Blessed Virgin and Saints. 13

in instituting the feasts she does in honour of the Saints ; and it is shown in the collect for St. Stephen's Day, which says : " O Lord ! give us grace to imitate that which we honour ". It is the constant tradition of the Church that the most essential part of devotion to the blessed in heaven is to profit by their example. Without this, all homage is vain. Whatever individual saint we are devout to, we must try to acquire that one's special virtues, and most of all are we bound to do this where the Queen of all Saints—the Virgin of virgins—is concerned. If we deeply revere—as every true Catholic does—the virginal chastity which enabled her to conceive the Son of God in her womb, we can duly express our veneration only by doing our best, according to our states of life, to imitate it in our own souls. So far does St. Ambrose go in his conviction of the power which the reverent imitation of Mary's virtue may confer on her true clients, that he says : " every chaste soul that keeps its purity and innocence untarnished *conceives the Eternal Wisdom in itself;* and is filled with God and His grace after the pattern of Mary ".

To women in especial does this duty of following the Blessed Virgin's example apply. Many portraits have been painted of Mary, by many artists, each painting her according to his own idea. There can, however, be only one true likeness of her : namely, a copy of her character as shown forth in the Gospels, the account of which forms a portrait drawn, if we may venture to say so, by the Holy Spirit Himself. And what is the character thus set before us in Scripture? This must be specially noted. It is neither Mary's high intercourse with God, nor her great and special graces, nor her power, that is dwelt upon in the Gospels. All these are kept in the background. What is brought before our notice is simply her ordinary every-day virtues, so to speak, that she may be a model for daily, familiar use. Now, the essence of Mary's character, as thus displayed, is her modesty and self-restraint. She never thinks of showing herself, though she was doubtless beautiful; nor of decking herself, though young; nor of exalting herself, though noble; nor of enriching herself, though poor. God alone is enough for her, and constitutes her whole happiness. Her delights are in retirement; and so little is she accustomed to the sight of man that she is troubled even at the appearance of an angel. Nevertheless, even in her trouble she *thinks:* she "considers within herself what manner of salutation this can be". Surprise and disturbance neither put her off her guard nor stifle reflection. Again, when her thought has taken form in resolution, she speaks—and speaks fearlessly. She has her chastity to guard; and so great is a true virgin's love of this that it makes her not only deaf to the promises of man, but proof—in reverence be it spoken—even against the promises of God. Mary, therefore, answers Gabriel—with no superfluous words, no curious or excited question or argument—but with

Devotion to the Blessed Virgin and Saints. 15

the calm and modest inquiry: "How shall this be done, because I know not man?" Blessed among women! to have spoken only in defence of her purity and to show her obedience! What a contrast and example, at this supreme moment of her life, to the kind of women who never control themselves or pause to reflect in disturbing circumstances or before grave decisions; but who let feeling and excitement get the better of them, pour themselves forth in vain and curious talk, or rush headlong into undertakings without knowledge or reflection!

And *after* this great event of the angel's mission, what is Mary's conduct? Is she either selfishly filled in thought with her own greatness, or anxious for the immediate display of her glory to the world? Just the contrary: wrapped in her deep lowliness, she is only surprised that God should have conferred such a dignity on *her;* and—mother of her Creator as she now is, whom all her fellow-creatures might well hasten to honour—she hurries off to her cousin Elizabeth, to rejoice with her over the grace that she and her husband have lately received. And even there, with her own relations, she speaks of the miracle that has been wrought within her only because she finds they have already been made aware of it by the Holy Ghost. Here is an example to people who no sooner receive a dignity or honour, or achieve a success of any description, than they must proclaim it to the world; who can keep nothing to themselves, but must live in the glare of publicity ; and who are so inwardly self-absorbed that they have hardly a thought left for the concerns of others.

Such, then—thoughtful and prudent, modest, self-restrained, humble, and unselfish—is this Virgin, of whom I repeat that we can never be her clients if we are not also her followers. St. Gregory Nazianzen has a beautiful saying : that " every man is the painter and sculptor of his own life". May all those of Mary's sex raise to her honour an image formed of their own lives, chiselled by themselves in her likeness! They may do this by forming their characters after her great example; by despising the vanities and frivolities of the world; and by strictly abjuring all customs—no matter how well received or sanctioned by society—that may be in the slightest degree contrary to charity or modesty. Mary will own that they truly honour her, and will unceasingly pray for them, when she sees them thus anxious to please her Son; and they will please her Son when he sees them like to the Mother He chose.

II.

ON THE CONCEPTION OF THE BLESSED VIRGIN.[1]

"Fecit mihi magna qui potens est."

THE subject of the Blessed Virgin's purity in her glorious Conception, which the Church celebrates and which will be treated of in all Catholic pulpits to-day, has for a long time exercised the greatest minds; and, of the many subjects that have to be expounded to the Faithful, it is perhaps one of the most difficult. I do not say this in the spirit of some orators, who exaggerate the poverty of their matter merely to exalt the rhetoric by which they intend to adorn it, for such a course would be utterly unworthy of a sacred theme; but because it is necessary, for clearly bringing out the real beauty and truth of Mary's Immaculate Conception, to begin by meeting some difficulties connected with the belief.

The consideration of that terrible sentence pronounced by the Apostle against mankind in general [2]— "*all* are dead: *all* have sinned: by the offence of one, unto *all* men's condemnation"[3]—is alone enough

[1] See Note p. 148, which forms an introduction to this Sermon.
[2] 2 Cor. v. 14. [3] Rom. v. 12, 16.

to make us wonder how an exception can be found to words of such wide application. But the universality of the curse is made still more plain by three different expressions used in Holy Scripture to represent the misfortune of our birth.

The Bible first announces a *supreme law* which it calls "the law of death": a verdict of guilt pronounced indifferently against *every* man born into the world. Who can be exempt from this?

Secondly, it tells us of a hidden and imperceptible *venom*, whose source was in Adam, and which infects each of his descendants terribly and inevitably. This was what St. Augustine called "*contagium mortis antiquæ*," and which made him say that the whole mass of the human race is contaminated. What preservative can be found against so subtle and penetrating a poison?

In the third place, we learn from Sacred Writ that all who breathe this infected air contract a stain which dishonours them, and destroys the image of God in them; and which thus makes them—as St. Paul says —"*naturally* children of wrath".[1] How hinder an evil that has actually become part of our nature for so long?

Such questions as these have disturbed the minds of some great thinkers—whose opinions, however, the Church does not condemn—by making it appear hard to prove Mary's perfect purity in her conception. It may be difficult, but I think we shall find it not im-

[1] Ephes. ii. 3.

On the Conception of the Blessed Virgin. 19

possible, to clear up doubts as to this great privilege of the Blessed Virgin.

It is quite true that a "law of death" exists, to which every person born is subject; but extraordinary people may always be dispensed from the most universal laws. There is undoubtedly an insidious and contagious poison that has infected our whole race; but we can sometimes escape contagion from a general epidemic by separating ourselves. We freely grant that an hereditary stain makes us natural enemies of God; but grace may anticipate nature. Hence, the line of thought to be followed, if we would prove an exception, is this: that we must find *dispensation* opposed to Law; *separation*, to Contagion; and *prevention*, to an expected natural evil. I propose to show that Mary was actually dispensed from the Law in question, by that supreme *Authority* which was so often exerted in her favour; that she was separated from universal contagion by the *Wisdom* which plainly disclosed Its unsearchable designs upon her, from before all time, by thus setting her apart; and that the Eternal *Love* of God so prevented her, where His anger was concerned, as to make her an object of mercy before she had time to become an object of wrath.

If we can understand it aright, we shall find that in her own marvellous Canticle she herself announces all this.[1] " He that is mighty hath done great things

[1] Luke i. 49.

to me." She speaks first of power, to give honour to the absolute Authority by Whom she is dispensed: *He that is mighty.* But what has this Almighty One done? " Ah ! " she declares, "*great things.*" It is clear that she here recognises her separation from others by the great and deep designs of the Wisdom that has called her apart. And what, we may ask, could possibly bring these great marvels to pass except the eternal Love of God,—ever active and ever fruitful,—without Whose intervention Omnipotence itself would not act, whilst Infinite Wisdom would keep Its thoughts unexpressed and bring forth nothing? It is this Love that does all things, and which consequently "*has done great things to me*": this alone makes God to pour Himself forth upon His creatures: this is the cause of all existence, the principle of all bestowal: and hence it was this effectual love which, in working Mary's Conception, *prevented* the threatened evil by sanctifying her from the very beginning.

By proving these three points, then, I shall both fully expound the text chosen, and explain and justify the high honour we pay to Mary in her most blessed Conception.

I.

It is decidedly a question whether, if it is the peculiar attribute of supreme authority to frame laws for whole nations, it is not even more perfectly char-

On the Conception of the Blessed Virgin. 21

acteristic of such authority to reserve for itself the right of dispensing from them where wisdom requires it; because the latter course, being extraordinary, seems to imply a higher degree of power and more independence than the former. If the majesty of Law is unequalled, and if to establish laws of his own is the highest and most sacred right of an absolute sovereign—which it undoubtedly is—then, when he makes those decrees themselves give way to his authority in special cases, he may be said with reason to *raise himself above his own supremacy.* This is God's mode of action when He works miracles, which are simply dispensations of things from the ordinary laws that He Himself had established; and which he performs to make his omnipotence more manifest. Hence, at first sight, it seems clear that the power of dispensation, or exception, is the most certain mark of authority.

On the other hand, equally strong arguments are put forward in favour of a different view. It is contended that because exceptions must always apply to an immensely smaller number than laws—or they could not be so called—and because a power exercised over numbers is surely more important than that exercised over a few, the establishing of universal Law is much the more absolutely authoritative work of the two. Again, it is urged that the continuous enforcement of *permanent* decrees is a truer sign of supreme power than the putting forth of *occasional* ones to counteract them—even though the latter act be in itself of a higher nature than the former.

The only way of reconciling these differences is to grant at once that the special characteristics of the highest authority appear equally in both forms of proceeding. This view is expressed by St. Thomas when he says that all Law comprises two things :—the *general commandment* and the *particular application* : as, for example, when Ahasuerus made a decree condemning *all* the Jews to death, but *excepted* Esther in applying that decree. In this rule of St. Thomas's, then, we have just what we are seeking :—a statement of the equal greatness of the two acts ; for the authority of *law-giving* is displayed in the " general commandment," and that of *dispensing* in the " particular application " ; and as it belongs to the maker of universal rules to judge of their suitability to special cases, it follows that the power of framing laws and that of dispensing from them are equally noble and inseparable attributes of a Supreme Ruler.

These principles being granted, we may proceed with our subject. I am told that there is a Decree of Death pronounced against all men, and that to make an exception, even though in favour of the Blessed Virgin herself, would be to violate the authority of law. But according to the rule just laid down, I may reply to this that, the Legislator's power having two sides, you would impugn His authority no less by denying His power to dispense with the application in this particular case, than by disputing His right to promulgate the general law in the first instance. St. Paul certainly declares in formal terms that "all are condemned"; but this need not disturb us; for in fully acknowledging the universal extent of the law, he in nowise excludes such reservations as the Sovereign may choose to make. By the authority of the law, incontestably, Mary was condemned like the rest of mankind; but by the grace of special reservations, made for her by the Sovereign's absolute power, she was dispensed from having the decree carried out in her case.

It may be objected that the whole strength of Law is weakened when its sacred dignity is sacrificed to the granting of dispensations. This is true, unless each dispensation is accompanied with three things:—that it is granted only to an eminent person; that it is founded on precedent; and that the honour of the Lawgiver is concerned in it. The first condition is due to the law itself, the second to the public, and the third to the Ruler; and without them an exception cannot justly be made. But where these conditions are combined, we may reasonably expect a special favour. Let us see if they were not so in the Holy Virgin.

Where exceptions are made, or dispensations granted, amongst equals—even though they be equals in greatness—one may justly fear for the consequences of deviation from the common rule. It must, however, be at once apparent that there can be no question of equality with any one where Mary is concerned; for in her case there is not only eminence, but *pre*-eminence. Is there a second *Mother of God?* Can there be another Virgin-mother to whom *her* prerogatives might possibly be extended? There can surely be no doubt in any minds that that glorious privilege of maternity, through which she has contracted an eternal alliance with God, places her in a quite peculiar rank that can suffer no sort of comparison.

From this very fact of her pre-eminence, it will of course be difficult to find a precedent for her exception from the law; and, in fact, it would be useless to seek for such in any other Saint. An example for God's dealings in this matter can actually be found only in Mary herself; and the observation of a not uncommon fact in all history will here help us.

It is very frequently the case that when Sovereigns have once begun bestowing favours in a certain direction they continue to bestow them there with ever-increasing liberality: benefits seem to attract, and make precedents for, one another; so that in a quarter where signal marks of favour have already been found, one may reasonably look for more. This principle is acknowledged by God Himself in the Gospels, when He says: "For to every one that hath shall be given";[1] which means that, in the order of His favours, a grace never goes alone, but is the pledge of many others.

[1] Matt. xxv. 29.

Now, apply this to the Blessed Virgin. Had she been subject throughout her life to ordinary rules we might easily believe her also "conceived in iniquity," in the same manner that others are. But when we find her enjoying a general dispensation from all common laws in every circumstance; when, according to Catholic faith and the teaching of the most approved Doctors, we see her not suffering in Child-birth, free from concupiscence, living a spotless life, and dying a painless death; when we learn that her reputed husband was but her guardian, her Son being the miraculous Child of Virginity, born through the power of the Holy Spirit instead of by the ordinary way of nature:—in short, when we find Mary *singular in everything:*—why should we expect her Conception to be the only part of her life that was *not* supernatural? It is much more logical to judge this event in the light of the rest, and to believe that it was a miracle in keeping with her whole life.

Thus, the two first conditions of a satisfactory dispensation — the superiority of the person concerned, and the existence of precedents in her favour —are clearly shown to be here fulfilled. I hope further to show that the third condition required is also present, and that the glory of the King—Jesus Christ Himself—is manifestly promoted by this dispensation.

It has been finely remarked that in certain circumstances "Princes themselves *gain what they give,* when their gifts are such as do them honour".[1] Now, Our Lord certainly honours Himself when He honours His Mother; and thus it may be truly said that He gains all He bestows upon her, because it is certainly grander for Him to give than for her to receive. However, a yet closer reason for our Divine Saviour's action in this matter lies in the fact that, having Himself *put on* this human flesh, for the express purpose of destroying that fatal decree which we have called " the law of death," it was—if we may so speak— only becoming to His own greatness to leave no possible place where it could claim to hold absolute sway. We must follow up this design, and see what victories it has won, in detail.

This law of spiritual death reigns over all men, and over all periods of each man's life. When we incur its penalties at an advanced age, Jesus Christ defeats it by His grace; the new-born infant groans under its tyranny, and He effaces it in baptism; it condemns the unborn child in the womb of his mother, so Our Saviour has chosen to free certain illustrious souls from its dominion there, by sanctifying them *before birth*, as in the case of St. John the Baptist.[2] But this terrible law goes yet farther back: it reigns over the very beginnings of man by seizing upon him the instant he is conceived [that is, animated]. Is Jesus

---

[1] Alaric, in *Cassiodorus*, Variar., lib. viii., Epist. xxiii.

[2] Also, according to the tradition of the Church, the Prophet Jeremias.

On the Conception of the Blessed Virgin. 27

Christ, the all-powerful conqueror, to be defeated in this one spot alone? Shall His sacred Blood—the divine remedy that *delivers* us from all evil—be ineffectual to *prevent* it? Surely not. Then, shall Its power remain for ever unused, and not be exerted on any of Christ's members? No:—the Saviour of mankind cannot fail to choose at least one among His creatures, even for the sake of His own glory, in whom to show forth the *full* power of His Precious Blood:—and what specially chosen creature should this be but His mother?

There is another aspect of the question which must be most carefully considered, for it makes us feel even more strongly that to doubt Mary's Immaculate Conception would be almost to depreciate the value of the Blood of Christ. This most sacred stream, we must never forget, not only had to flow over Mary, as over the whole race, to redeem her; but it was to have *Its human source* in her body. This is a wonderful and overpowering thought; but it is absolutely true, or Christ would not be God and man; and, being true, can we doubt that Our Lord's honour requires the very channel whence He was to receive *His own* Blood to be purified in its beginning? But to bring this about Mary's Son must hinder the law of death from taking effect in her, at the first moment she becomes a living person:—that is, at the instant of her conception. Thus He pays due honour to the Life-giving Stream Itself, by honouring the spot whence it was to spring.

We must not, then, look for Mary's name in the catalogue of those condemned by the fatal decree: it has been blotted out simply by that Divine Blood drawn from her own chaste veins, and applied by her Son—to His own true glory—with fullest efficacy for her benefit.

The three conditions are thus shown to be complied with, and I have proved my first point:—that the Blessed Virgin was justly dispensed, by the rightful authority, from suffering under the general condemnation.

Tertullian has said that, because of the Supreme Majesty of God, it is not only glorious for His creatures to consecrate their lives to His service, but that it is even right for them to offer Him "the submission of flattery": *Non tantum obsequi ei debeo, sed et adulari:*[1] —in other words, that we must not only obey His direct commandments, but keep every movement of our being so completely dependent on His will that we are ready to comply with the smallest sign of His pleasure. What Tertullian says of God Himself, our common Father, I would say of His Church, Mother of all the Faithful:—that we should be ready, as good Christians, not only to follow her precepts, but to respond to the slightest expression of her desires. Now, she does not compel our obedience by placing belief in the Immaculate Conception of Mary amongst her Articles of Faith which we must accept under pain

---

[1] Tertull., *de Jejun.*, n. 13.

On the Conception of the Blessed Virgin. 29

of sin; but by the very Feast of to-day she *invites* us to acknowledge it. Let us, then, say with perfect and fearless confidence that the Blessed Virgin was conceived without spot; and, in so doing, honour Jesus Christ in His Mother :—believing that He wrought a special work in her conception because she was chosen from among all others to conceive *Him*.

2.

It is the very fact of this peculiar relation of Mother and Son between Mary and Christ—the fact that He Himself was *conceived in her womb*—which is the great argument for our second point to be proved: the belief that His Wisdom *separated* her in a peculiar manner from the universal contagion that all other souls contract when united to "flesh of sin". And I say advisedly "in a peculiar manner": for, observe, *all* who are saved by Baptism, actual or of desire— before or after Christ's coming—are *separated*, by being freed from the effects of the taint they have contracted, through grace. In fact, God has carried out this principle of "separation" in many forms from the beginning of all things: Holy Writ speaks of His "separating" one part of the universe after another from the first-formed matter; and, just as He first divided earth, sea, and sky from the shapeless mass, so He now parts the faithful from the mass of criminal humanity by that grace which is the work of the Holy Spirit, who has chosen them out from all eternity.

What else but this does St. Paul mean, when he speaks of "Him, who separated me from my mother's womb and called me by His grace?"[1] Hence, the *fact* of the Blessed Virgin's separation is common to the whole body of the elect; it is the *nature* of it that is peculiar to herself, on account of the *cause*.

We may take, as a help towards considering this mystery in detail, some beautiful words of Eusebius, in his second Homily on Our Lord's Nativity. He says, speaking of Mary's bliss in having conceived her Saviour: "Thou hast deserved to receive *first* Him whose coming was promised throughout all ages; and thou alone dost possess *by a peculiar gift* the joy that is common to all men".[2] If Jesus Christ is a *common possession*—if the Mysteries of His Life were wrought for the whole world—in what way could the Blessed Virgin possess Him "alone"? His death was a public sacrifice, His Blood the price of all sins, His preaching the doctrine for all nations: the fact that, directly the Divine Infant was born, the Jews were called to Him by angels and the Gentiles by a star, clearly shows that He belongs to the entire earth. The whole world has a right to the Son of God, because God's goodness bestowed Him on all. Nevertheless — O wondrous dignity of Mary!—amid this universal ownership she has a peculiar right of

---

[1] Gal. i. 15.

[2] Per tot sæcula promissum, prima suscipere mereris adventum; et commune mundi gaudium, peculiari munere sola possides.

On the Conception of the Blessed Virgin. 31

possessing Him alone, because she can claim Him as her *Son* :—a title which no other creature can share. God Himself and Mary, *only*, can call the Saviour "Son"; and by this most sacred tie Jesus Christ gives Himself to her in such a manner that the general treasure of all men may be truly called her particular property : *sola possides*.

But, it may be said, however glorious such a separation may be, what effect will it have in sanctifying her conception? To answer this question we must show that Our Saviour's own Conception exerts a secret influence over that of the Blessed Virgin, to which it imparts grace and sanctity ; and we shall do this best by first calling to mind a truth full of comfort to all Christians :—namely, that the life of the Saviour of souls has a particular relation to every part of our own lives, that it may sanctify them. The Apostle expresses this truth when he says : " Jesus Christ died and rose again, that He might be Lord *both of the dead and the living*".[1] Observe the relation :—the Saviour's life sanctifies ours ; our death is consecrated by His. And it is the same throughout : He clothed Himself with our weakness, which strengthens us in infirmity—He has felt our troubles, which consoles us in affliction and makes it holy and profitable to us : in short, Christ took upon Himself *all that we are;* and there is a secret relation between Him and us which causes our sanctification. And whence comes

[1] Rom. xiv. 9.

this marvellous communication between His states and ours? The Apostle would reply that it comes from the fact that the Saviour, dying and suffering, *belongs to us: He gives us* His death and His sufferings; and in them we find graces that impart sanctity to our own, by making them like His. All Christians may say this; but there is *one* relation to Him which the Blessed Virgin only can claim :—she alone has the right to say " The Redeemer, *when He was conceived as man,* gave Himself to me by a peculiar title, and in such a manner that His conception breathed sanctity into mine by its secret influence ".

This, then, is the argument for Mary's being separated from the universal taint in her conception :— that she was chosen to be the parent of God made man; that He was given to her by the Heavenly Father, to conceive, and to bear within her sacred womb; and that whilst she thus bore Him—though for the rest of His life He was to belong equally to all men—she had a right of peculiar possession, as the Mother who had conceived Him : "*peculiari munere sola possides*". Hence, it was surely just that Our Lord should do something singular for her who had been set apart by Divine wisdom to bear this singular relation to Him :—that the office for which she was destined should draw down a peculiar blessing of sanctification on her own conception? We must, then, acknowledge Mary as *separated* by an extraordinary operation of the Son of God. Divine

Wisdom Itself ordained the separation, because of the peculiar tie between her and her Son which made it just for her to share His privileges.

We see, further, that the Blessed Virgin in her separateness has something in common with all men and something peculiar to herself: for, as was said above, we are all separated from the mass by belonging to Christ. But Our Lord has a double tie with Mary:— one as *Saviour*, in common with the whole race; the other as *Son*, by which He belongs only to her. By the first tie, she is bound to be parted from the mass like all other men; by the second, she is bound to be set apart from it in an extraordinary manner. In this work, we behold the Divine Wisdom once more bringing order out of confusion as formerly in the case of the elements. Here is a mass of criminal humanity, from which a creature has to be separated in order to be made mother of her Creator. Jesus Christ is her Saviour:—hence she must be separated in the same way as others; but Jesus Christ is also her Son, and therefore she must be separated *from* others:—if others are delivered from evil, she must be preserved from it, so that its very course may be hindered. How can this be, except by some more special communication of her Son's privileges? He is exempt from sin:—Mary must be exempt also. Thus Wisdom has separated her from others; but still she must not be confounded with her Son, since she is of necessity infinitely beneath Him. How, then, are we to distinguish between them? In this way:—Jesus Christ is exempt from sin by nature, Mary by grace; Jesus Christ by right, Mary by privilege and indulgence.

It is clear, then, that she may say of her separation " He that is mighty hath done *great things* to me"; and we may now go on to see how grace filled her so completely that the anger which threatens every child of Adam could not influence her conception, because it was forestalled by merciful love.

3.

If Holy Scripture tells us that the Son of God, in taking our flesh, also took upon Him all our infirmities, sin alone excepted; if the plan that He had formed of making Himself like unto us caused Him not to disdain hunger, or thirst, or fear, or sadness, or a thousand other weaknesses that seem unworthy of His dignity:—then still more must we believe that He was deeply imbued with that just and holy love, impressed upon us by nature itself, for those to whom we owe life. This truth is, indeed, evident; but I wish to show here that it was that special love which *prevented* the Blessed Virgin in her happy conception— and I will explain my meaning fully.

I shall consider the filial love that Our Saviour bore to Mary under two conditions:—namely, *in* the Incarnation, and *before* the Incarnation, of the Divine Word. No Christian can find it hard to believe that it existed in the Incarnation, for as it was by this fact that Mary became the Mother of God, it was also in the accomplishment of that august mystery that God acquired the feelings of a Son for Mary. But it is not so easy to understand how filial love for His holy Mother can have been found in God before He became incarnate, as the Son of God is her Child only on account of the humanity He took upon Him. Nevertheless, if we look farther back we shall discover that love which "prevented" Mary by the profusion of its gifts, already existing; and the understanding of this truth will prove the love of God for our nature.

There are three things that distinguish the Blessed Virgin from all mothers:—she gave birth to the Bestower of grace; her Son—differing in this from all others—could put forth His full powers from the first moment of His life; and, which is most wonderful of all, she was the mother of a Son Who existed before her. These three facts produce three magnificent effects in Mary. As her Son is the Bestower of grace He gives her a very large share of it; as He is able to act from the moment of His birth, He need not delay His liberality towards her, but begins to shower His gifts the instant she has conceived Him; lastly, having a Son Whose Being preceded hers, she is so miraculously placed that the love of that Son can go before her even in her own conception, and make that event innocent: it was indeed her right that such a Son should so benefit her.

This truth is made still clearer through a doctrine

held by some of the Fathers about the way in which the Son of God has loved the Blessed Virgin from eternity. They have drawn the doctrine from something that we must have often wondered at ourselves :— from the way in which God, throughout Holy Scripture, appears to delight—if we may say so—in behaving as man : how He actually copies our actions, our manners and customs, our feelings and our passions. Now He will say, by the mouth of His prophets, that His Heart is seized with compassion ; then, again, that it is inflamed with anger :—that He is appeased, that He "repents Him," that He is glad or sorrowful. What means this mystery? Does it become a God to act thus? For the Incarnate Word to speak in this fashion seems natural, for He was man ; but for God, *before* He was man, to act and speak as men do seems truly strange. It may be reasonably suggested that He does it to bring His Sovereign Majesty within our reach ; but the Fathers find a more mysterious reason for it. They tell us that God, having once resolved to unite Himself to our nature, judged it not beneath Him to adopt all its feelings beforehand :—nay, that He made them His own, and might even be said to have *studied* how to conform Himself to them.

If it is not irreverent to illustrate so great a mystery by a familiar example, I would suggest a parallel in the ordinary conduct of a man who is expecting a civil or military appointment. He has not got it ; but he prepares for it by adopting in advance all the habits of

On the Conception of the Blessed Virgin. 37

mind that are proper to it; and he tries in good time to acquire either the gravity of a judge or the generous courage of a soldier. God has determined to become man : He has not done so in the days of the Prophets, but it is certain that He will. Hence, we are not to wonder if He takes pleasure in appearing to the Patriarchs and Seers in human guise, by speaking and acting like a man before He has become one. And why? Tertullian answers admirably :—*to prepare for the Incarnation.* He Who is to stoop so low as to assume our nature, is serving (with all reverence be it spoken) His apprenticeship, by conforming to our ways. " He accustoms Himself little by little to being man; and learns from the beginning what He is to be in the end." [1]

Let none, then, think that God awaited His coming on earth to have a filial love for the Blessed Virgin. That He had resolved to become man was enough to make him adopt a man's feelings; and if He took those upon Him, would He be likely to forget the feelings of a Son—the most natural and human of them all? Hence He has always loved Mary as His Mother, and looked upon her as such from the first moment she was conceived : could He, therefore, look upon her with anger? Would sin in her be consistent with so many graces, vengeance with love, enmity with union? Sin, it is true, has raised a wall of separation

---

[1] " Ediscens jam inde a primordio, jam inde hominem, quod erat futurus in fine."—Lib. ii., adv. Marcion, n. 27.

between God and man—has established a natural enmity; but may not Mary say with the Psalmist: *In Deo meo transgrediar murum?*[1] Yes: she will not be shut off by a barrier—she will pass over the wall—and how? " *In the name of my God* :—of that God Who, being my Son, is mine by a peculiar right: that God Who has loved me as His mother from the first moment of my life: that God Whose all-powerful and *prevenient* Love has turned aside the wrath that threatens every child of Eve."

Such is the work that has been wrought in the Blessed Virgin; and we may, therefore, safely cry: " O Mary, miraculously dispensed, peculiarly separated, mercifully prevented, help our weakness by thy prayers, and obtain for us sinners this grace :—that we may so forestall by penance the punishment due to our sins, as to be at last received into the Kingdom of eternal peace, with the Father, Son, and Holy Ghost ".

[1] Ps. xvi. 32.

III.

MARY A FORESHADOWING OF CHRIST.

(*Preached on a Feast of Mary's Nativity.*)

"Nox præcessit, dies autem appropinquavit" (Rom. xiii. 12).

ART and nature alike produce their works gradually, and God Himself does the same. The pencil precedes the brush ; the architect's design maps out the building to come :—there is no *chef d'œuvre* accomplished in the world but goes through its preliminary stages ; whilst nature, in the development of her designs, often tries her 'prentice hand in ways that seem almost like play.

The work in which our Maker most remarkably follows the same plan is that of the Incarnation, for the sake of which He declared that He would " move the heaven and the earth "[1] :—this being His One Work above all others. Although its fulfilment was not to be till " the middle of years,"[2] He nevertheless began it from the beginning of the world. The natural and the written Law—ceremonies and sacrifices—priest-

[1] Agg. ii. 7.   [2] Habac. iii. 2.

hood and prophets—were all, speaking reverently, merely *sketches* or *outlines* of the "perfect Man, Christ Jesus". They are called by an ancient writer *Christi rudimenta;* and the grand work itself was reached only through a succession of images and figures that served as preparatory designs. But when the time comes close for the Mystery, God plans something yet more excellent than these:—He forms the blessed Mary, that He may represent Jesus Christ to us more naturally than before. He is about to send Him on earth, and so combines all His most beautiful characteristics in the person of her who is to be His mother.

Tertullian,[1] contemplating and discussing the marvellous interest that God displayed in the act of forming man from "the slime of the earth," seeks for some explanation of the immense pains that He bestowed on the work. He declares himself unable to believe that He put forth so much power, to mould so base a material, without some further great end in view: and this end, he finally concludes, is nothing less than *Jesus Christ,* Who is to be born of the race of man, and Whom God, therefore, chooses to typify to us by His manner of forming the first members of that race. *Quodcumque limus exprimebatur, Christus cogitabatur homo futurus.*

If this idea is true:—if God, when He created the first Adam, meant to trace out the second; if He

[1] *De Resur. carn.*, n. 6.

Mary a Foreshadowing of Christ. 41

formed our first father so carefully with Jesus our Saviour in view, and because His Divine Son was to spring from him after many generations:—surely to-day, when we see Mary—who was to bear Christ within her womb—come into the world, we may conclude that in creating *her* God was thinking of our Lord and working for Him alone? Hence there is no cause for surprise either in His having formed her so carefully or in His endowing her with so many graces as He did: for to make her worthy of His Son He models her upon that Son Himself. Intending soon to bestow on us His Word Incarnate, on the day of Mary's nativity He gives us an outline—I might almost say a *beginning*—of Jesus Christ, in one who, though a creature, is in some sort a living expression of His own perfections. Thus we may truly apply to such a day the Apostle's beautiful words: " The night has passed and the day is at hand ".

The Redeemer of mankind, besides being in Himself an inexhaustible Fount of Love, must necessarily possess the two qualities of exemption from sin and fulness of grace. He must be innocent to purify us from our crimes, and full of grace to enrich our poverty ; for these qualities are inseparable from the character and office of the Saviour. When God formed the Blessed Virgin on the pattern of the Sun of Justice, some of the rays by which He was to dispel our darkness were permitted to shine forth in her, though only in a degree that faintly foreshadowed the brilliant light they were to shed over the world when they should stream in their fulness from Jesus Christ Himself; and hence it came that she was endowed with the very qualities that were to form an intrinsic part of Her Divine Son's human nature, especially with these two of *innocence* and *fulness of grace*. We are here to consider shortly both the cause and the manner of Mary's likeness to her Son in these particular points :—and, first, the special relation of her innocence to His.

In the whole teaching of the Gospels there is nothing more touching than God's gentle and loving way of treating His reconciled enemies : that is, converted sinners. He is not satisfied with blotting out our stains and washing away our filth : to His infinite goodness it is but a little thing that our sins should do us no harm :—He would have them actually profit us. He draws out of them such benefits for our soul that we even feel constrained to bless our very transgressions, and to cry with the Church : *O Felix culpa !* [1] His grace seems to struggle with our sins for the upper hand ; and St. Paul says that it even pleases Him to make grace abound more where sin has abounded.[2] In fact, He receives penitent sinners back with so much love that innocence itself might almost be said to have cause for complaint—or at least for some jealousy—at the sight of it. The

---

[1] Blessing of the Paschal Candle on Holy Saturday.
[2] Rom, v. 20,

Mary a Foreshadowing of Christ. 43

extreme gentleness with which He treats them, if their regret for sin be but real, appears to do away with all further need for regret. Let but one sheep stray from His side, and it seems to become dearer to Him than all the others who remained constant; like the father in the parable, His heart melts over His returned prodigal rather than over the elder, faithful brother.

We seem, indeed, at first sight to have ground for saying that the penitent sinner has the advantage over the just who have not sinned :—that restored virtue may triumph over innocence preserved; nevertheless, it is not so. We may never doubt that innocence is a privileged state; and if there were no other reason for maintaining this it would be enough to remember that Jesus Christ chose that state for Himself. Observe the terms in which the great Apostle declares His Divine Master's innocence:[1] *Talis decebat ut esset nobis pontifex:* " It was fitting that we should have a high priest, holy, innocent, undefiled, separated from sinners, and made higher than the heavens : Who needeth not to offer sacrifices for His own sins "—but, being holiness itself, expiates sin. Must not the Son of God, then, have dearly loved the innocence that He took for His own lot? No: His tender feelings for converted sinners does not place them above holy souls that have never been stained by sin. Only, just as we feel the blessing of

[1] Hebr. vii. 26,

health most keenly on recovering from a long illness, though we would far rather have been spared the illness and kept our strength unbroken; or, again, as a lovely mild day in the midst of a hard winter is peculiarly enjoyed from its unexpectedness, yet is by no means so pleasureable as a long mild season would have been :—so, humanly speaking, we may understand how Our Lord lavishes tenderness on freshly converted sinners, who are His latest conquest; yet nevertheless has a more ardent love for His early friends, the Just. We may, indeed—to go higher for an explanation—describe His whole attitude, as regards the "one sinner that repenteth" and the "ninety-nine just," very shortly and simply by keeping in mind His twofold nature, which causes Him to feel differently as Son of God and as Saviour of men.

Though Jesus Christ, as Son of God, may take pleasure in seeing at His feet a sinner who has returned to the right path, yet, being Himself *essential Sanctity* He must love the innocence that has never strayed with a stronger love; for as it is nearer to, and more perfectly imitates, His own infinite holiness, He cannot help honouring it by closer familiarity. Whatever favour the tears of a penitent may find in His eyes, they can never equal the pure charm of a holiness ever-faithful to Him. But when God becomes man to save us from our sins He, *as our Saviour*, comes to seek the guilty: for them He lives, because to them He was sent.

Mary a Foreshadowing of Christ. 45

How does He Himself describe the object of His mission? "*I came not to seek the Just,*"[1] that is to say: "Though they may be the most noble and worthy of My friendship, My commission does not extend to them. As Saviour, I am to seek the lost; as Physician, the sick; as Redeemer, those who are captive." Hence it is that He loves only the society of such as these—because to them alone He was sent into the world. The angels, who never fell, may approach Him as Son of God:—that is the prerogative of innocence; but, in His quality of *Saviour*, He gives the preference to sinners; just as a doctor who, as a man, will prefer to hold intercourse with the healthy, would nevertheless, as a physician, rather tend the sick. Here is an evangelical interpretation of the whole mystery which is full of comfort for sinners like us. At the same time, however, it tells strongly in favour of Mary's perpetual purity; for if the Son of God loves innocence so intensely, could it be that He should find none on earth? Of course He has it Himself in the highest degree of perfection; but shall He not have the satisfaction of finding here below something like Himself, or at least slightly approaching His own spotlessness? We cannot believe that He should have to live entirely among sinners without the consolation of intercourse with one spotless soul, and who should this be but His mother? If He must spend His life in seeking sinners throughout the

[1] Matt. ix. 13.

whole range of Palestine, and find criminals wherever He turns outside His home, surely just within it He may find wherewith to feast His soul on the lasting beauty of unsullied holiness?

True:—Our Lord not only never shows contempt for sinners by banishing them from His presence, but actually calls them to the highest offices in His kingdom. He entrusts the charge of His flock to a Peter who has denied Him ; He puts the publican Matthew at the head of the Evangelists ; and makes Paul, the chief of persecutors, into the first of preachers:—*not the just and innocent, but the converted sinners, have the first places.* Nevertheless, He does not take His holy mother from among their ranks : between her and others there must be a difference of a special kind, and to which careful attention must be paid ; for it is an essential and fundamental part of the subject I am treating.

Christ chose the former—the penitent sinners whom He put in high places—*for others ;* and He chose Mary *for Himself.* For others : " All things are yours, whether it be Paul, or Apollo, or Cephas ".[1] Mary for Himself: " *My beloved to me, and I to Him* [2] : He is my Only One and I am His only one ; He is my Son, and I am His mother ". He drew those whom He chose for others from the ranks of sinners that they might the better announce His mercy and the remission of sins. His whole design was to restore

[1] 1 Cor. iii. 22. [2] 2 Cant. ii. 16.

confidence in souls that were cast down by guilt; and who could better preach divine mercy than those who themselves furnished striking examples of it? Who could say with greater effect that it was "a faithful saying . . . that Jesus Christ came into this world to save sinners," than a St. Paul who could add "*of whom I am the chief*"?[1] It was just as if he had said to the sinner whom he wanted to win: "Fear not; I know the hand of the physician I would send you to. He Himself has sent me to tell you how He cured me:—how easily—how tenderly; and to promise you the same happiness":—as St. Augustine said in after years.[2] It was, then, a truly wise means of drawing sinners to God to have His mercy proclaimed to them by men who had so deeply experienced it. St. Paul teaches this plainly: "For this cause," he says, "I have obtained mercy; that in me first Jesus Christ shall show forth all patience, for the information of them that shall believe unto life everlasting".[3] Thus we see why God honours reconciled sinners with the first offices in the Church:—for the instruction of the Faithful.

But if this was the course He pursued with those whom He appointed for the good of others, it was not His mode of proceeding where the extraordinary, privileged, and cherished being was concerned whom He created for Himself only: with her whom He

---

[1] 1 Tim. i. 15.   [2] Serm. clxxvi., n. 4, tom. v., col. 841.
[3] 1 Tim. i. 16.

chose for His Mother. In her case He did—not, as when He chose His Apostles and Ministers, what was profitable to the salvation of all—but what was most sweet and satisfying to *Him*, and most for His own glory. She was to possess none but Him for her own, and He none but her, and therefore He would have her innocent from the beginning. The gift of perfect innocence, of course, may not be too freely lavished on our corrupt nature; but for God to bestow it on His own Mother alone cannot be called lavish; whilst to refuse it even to her would be restricting it too far.

We may, then, I repeat, consider that with Mary's birth a preliminary ray of the full light of Christ is shed on the world: as St. Peter Damian beautifully puts it: *Nata Virgine surrexit Aurora.*[1] But, perfectly as her innocence foreshadows His, we are not to suppose that it puts her on a par with Him; for it belongs to Jesus by right, to Mary only by privilege; to Jesus by nature, to Mary only by grace and indulgence; in Jesus we honour the very source of all innocence, in Mary only a stream from that source. Mary's innocence, in short, is but the outflowing on to a specially chosen *creature*, of Christ's own freedom from sin: and her spotlessness possesses a quality in which it differs from the purity of other innocent creatures, which is peculiarly comforting and encouraging to us. Innocence of life in ordinary human beings is rather apt to

[1] Sermon xi. (in Assumpt. B. Mar. Virg.).

be a reproach to those of bad life, and to have a repelling effect on the guilty by seeming to condemn them. In Mary, however, the Divine Innocence from which hers is derived shines forth with its own character: and that character does not consist in a purity that seems to judge or reproach criminals, but in one that exists only to be their life and salvation. Hence this holy and innocent creature never repels or discourages us by the sight of her faultlessness, as she uses it only to raise and win pardon for us; whilst by the shining light of her purity we may see to cleanse away our own offences.

Then, having done this, we may become spiritually rich by filling our emptiness at the fountain of those innumerable graces, the possession of which—as I said above—constitutes the second special likeness of Mary to her Son. To treat adequately of these graces is, however, more difficult than to discuss her innocence; for the mere recollection of her dignity as Mother of God makes it easy to realise her exemption from sin. But when it comes to setting forth the fulness of her graces, the mere thought of their number is overpowering, and one knows not where to begin. What I propose, therefore, is to indicate what their extent must be by considering the principle whence they all sprang, rather than to attempt describing them individually.

This principle, of course, is the same as that of every grace and virtue that has adorned the whole human race from the beginning: the fact of Jesus Christ's union with mankind. But His union with His Mother is so much closer than with any other creature that it must naturally result in her being much more richly endowed with grace than any one else: indeed, we can hardly place any limit to the endowments that such a bond as hers with her Son would entitle her to. Had this bond been only such a one as ordinary mothers have with their children it must have brought her innumerable gifts from God; but we must remember what is too often overlooked, that the tie between Mary and Christ was something beyond that of mere parent and child, in two ways.

First, it was a *spiritual* tie; for Mary—as we are specially told in Holy Scripture—conceived her Son by Faith. When she went to visit St. Elizabeth the latter cried: "Blessed art thou *that hast believed* ——!"[1] which was as much as to say, "thou art a mother, indeed, but it is thy *faith* that has made thee so". From this the Fathers of the Church have unanimously argued that the Blessed Virgin's union with her Son began in the exactly opposite way to that of ordinary mothers. *They* are united to their children corporally at first, conceiving them naturally, according to the flesh; but *she* conceived hers purely by the Spirit, apart from nature, and had no corporal union with Him till after her act of faith and obedience had enabled her to receive Him within her: *Prius concepit*

[1] Luke i. 43.

mente quam corpore, St. Augustine says.[1] Thus, its spiritual nature is the first great distinction between Mary's motherhood and that of other women.

The second difference between them is that Christ chose to be miraculously born without a human father, and thus to receive His sacred flesh and blood from her alone when He became man. Hence His tie with her was not merely that of an only Son, but of an only Son to Whom she stood—humanly speaking—in the place of both parents, and from Whom she therefore had the right to a double share of His holy affections.

Here, then, we have plainly set before us the Blessed Virgin's title to the " fulness of grace," modelled on that of Christ Himself, that I have claimed for her ; and from the greatness of her claim we may judge of the liberality with which it would be granted. When we see so clearly what she is to be to Him, we find no room left for doubting that He will send her into the world not only free from sin, but actually endowed with every virtue, that she may thus truly shadow forth, as a faithful image, the Messias to Whom she is to give birth when the time is ripe. Christ, we must never forget, is the Author of His own Mother's existence ; and if even ordinary man is formed on the model of the Sacred Humanity, how much nearer to it must not that Mother's likeness be?

[1] Sermon ccxv., n. 4, tom. v., col. 950

IV.

ON THE NATIVITY OF THE BLESSED VIRGIN.

(*Being two of Bossuet's Sermons combined.*)

"Quis, putas, puer iste erit?" (St. Luke i. 66).

BEFORE the birth of Our Lord, all good men who lived in expectation of Israel's Redeemer incessantly longed for His coming. They ardently desired that the Eternal Father should hasten the hour of sending them their Deliverer; and the transports of joy with which they would have greeted the smallest sign that that hour was approaching may be well imagined by us. Suppose them, then, to have known when the Blessed Virgin was born that she was to be the Saviour's Mother, what may we not conclude would have been their delight? Even as those races that worship the sun rejoice at the sight of his herald, the dawn, so would the men of faith in Israel have been enraptured at the thought of beholding the glorious birthday of her who was to usher in the coming of the "Desired of all Nations". We who come after them can understand their feelings. Moved by reverence for Him Who chose her for His Mother, we come to-day to do

On the Nativity of the Blessed Virgin.

honour to this newly-risen star : to deck her cradle—not, indeed, with actual lilies and roses—but with the holy desires and heartfelt praise that are the true flowers of the Spirit.

I shall best express what I have to say of Mary's Nativity by arranging my subject under certain definite heads. I shall try to show that her first great advantage as the Mother of Jesus Christ will be her lasting blessedness in loving Him with a quite unequalled affection, and her second prerogative the corresponding love—incapable of comparison—that He will bear to her. I hope further to prove that she will possess a third wonderful privilege in the fact that her union with Jesus will unite her also in the closest manner with the Eternal Father; and finally to explain how this union will confer on her the Motherhood of the Faithful, who are at once children of the Father and brethren of the Son.

The subject is great and difficult ; but I enter upon it with confidence in the helping grace of the Blessed Trinity; for is not Mary daughter of the Father, mother of the Son, and spouse of the Holy Ghost?

I.

To begin with the two first-named privileges :—my first point is that this new-born maiden is unspeakably blessed in being predestined to experience such exceeding love for Him Who is alone really worthy of our hearts.

We all acknowledge that the highest gift ever given by God to His saints is love for the Lord Jesus. From the beginning of all ages, before His coming, He was the delight of the Patriarchs. Abraham, Isaac, and Jacob could hardly contain their joy at only remembering that He was to be born of their race. How, then, can Mary, from whose very flesh He is to spring—who is to gaze on Him sleeping in her arms, or feeding from her virginal breast—do otherwise than feel her whole being dilate with love of Him? And afterwards, when with His first infant lisp He begins to call her "Mother"; when, as His childish speech develops a little, she hears Him offer His earliest tribute of praise to God His Father; and when, later, she sees Him in the privacy of home moving about, eagerly obedient to her lightest word:—how burning will not be the ardour of her love?

But, besides the grace of loving Our Lord, another great gift of God is to be able to *think* much of Him. We well know that His Name is honey to the lips, light to the eyes, and a flame to the heart:[1] God has conferred a nameless grace on every one of His words and actions, to think on which is Eternal life. Those who think of them often, undoubtedly find unspeakable comfort in so doing. In this practice consisted the whole sweetness of Mary's life: we see from the Gospels that she incessantly went over and over again in her thoughts whatever her Son said to her and

[1] St. Bernard, Serm. xv. in Cant., n. 6, tom. i., col. 1311.

On the Nativity of the Blessed Virgin. 55

whatever was said to her about Him : *Maria autem conservabat omnia verba hæc in corde suo.*[1] Only by depriving her of life itself could one have obliterated these thoughts from her heart, for they formed part of her very life-blood. If even ordinary mothers have their interests bound up in those of their sons how much more must Mary's have been so bound? How intensely must she have admired His life, been charmed by His words, suffered in His passion, loved with His love, and rejoiced in His glory! And when He returned to His Father, what must have been her impatience to go to Him?

St. Thomas[2] says that the inequality amongst the Blessed in Heaven will consist in this :—that those who have most ardently desired the Divine presence in this world will enjoy it most abundantly in the next, because the sweetness of enjoyment is in proportion to the desire. By the burning impatience of St. Paul, who so craved for his Lord's embrace in eternity that he ardently wished to "*be dissolved* to be with Christ,"[3] we may judge somewhat of what would be the feelings and longings of Christ's mother. Even Tobias's mother felt terribly one year's absence from her son :[4] and what an immeasurable distance between her love and that of Mary! What, then, must be the place in Heaven to be attained by the Blessed Infant round whom our thoughts are centring to-day? If

[1] Luke ii. 19. [2] I. Part., Quaest. xii., art. v.
[3] Phil. i. 23. [4] Tob. v. 23 *et seq.*

her greatness is to be according to the measure of her desires she must surpass all the hierarchies of angels; for her only fitting place amongst the heavenly hosts will be close to the throne of her much-loved Son Himself, there to share the most intimate secrets of His heart, and to exert her all-powerful influence with Him for ever:—there to offer those petitions for us which His filial love will make Him unable to refuse.

This thought brings us naturally to consider the other side of our great subject:—that Love with which the Son of God honours the Blessed Virgin. If it is difficult to treat the first affection as it deserves, it seems well-nigh impossible to say anything adequate of the second; for in as far as Our Lord necessarily surpasses Mary in all other things, so He must be far greater in His capacity of Son than she in that of Mother. The only suitable, as well as the most moving, way of treating such a subject is to see what can be found about it in the Gospels:—as, indeed, may be said of all subjects; for one word of Holy Scripture has more power over the soul than all that human eloquence can produce. What, then, can we discover in the Sacred writings that will help towards some realisation of Christ's feelings for His Mother? Nothing, I think, to equal the wonderful account of His deep love of *human nature* itself. It is worth while to make a short digression for considering this.

The manner in which Our Saviour took upon Himself *everything* belonging to man—sin alone excepted —even to our greatest infirmities, is an unanswerable argument against those unpardonable heretics who, having dared to deny the reality of His sacred flesh, necessarily denied the reality of His sufferings and human passions. By doing this they deprived themselves of the greatest possible consolation; for, whatever sort of trouble we may be afflicted with, we may always remember that we have the honour of enduring it in our Divine Master's company, when we know that all His human weaknesses were *actually real.* If a man suffers from want, let Him think of His Saviour's hunger and thirst, and extreme indigence. Is he injured in reputation? His Lord was "despised and rejected of men". Does some depressing infirmity keep hold of him? Christ "suffered unto death". Or, again, we may be overpowered by a crushing sense of weariness:—then we can go to the garden of olives, and there behold Our Lord in a state of such fear, sadness, and overwhelming oppression that He actually sweats blood and water at the mere thought of His trial. No one has ever heard of such a thing as this in the case of any other person; therefore we may safely say that never did any human being possess feelings so tender, so delicate, and so strong, as Our Saviour's: though they were kept under extreme control because of being perfectly subject to the Will of His Father.

Now, the relation that all this bears to the special point under consideration is twofold. First—(as we have already seen in connection with the subject of Mary's immaculate conception)—the thought that Christ took upon Himself, so wholly and sincerely, such infirmities of our race as might even seem unworthy of Him, makes us certain that He cannot possibly have failed to adopt the universal and natural feeling of filial devotion towards her who had bestowed His human life upon Him. Next, if we remember how deeply the special acuteness of His feelings would make Him love His Mother on even ordinary grounds, we shall the better understand what must have been His affection for such a mother as Mary, in return for such gifts as He had received from her. It is not too bold to say that, as man, He owed to her—besides life itself—a portion of His glory, and the purity of His flesh.

This statement, though perhaps a little startling at first sight, is none the less true; neither does it in any way detract from the glory of the Master. It may be well proved from an argument set forth by St. Augustine in many fine passages of his writings, but especially in his books against Julian. This great man, from the lamentable fact that concupiscence has a share in all ordinary births, draws the conclusion that that accursèd thing—corrupting whatever it comes near—so poisons the matter whence our bodies are formed that the flesh composed of it necessarily con-

On the Nativity of the Blessed Virgin. 59

tracts corruption. Hence, the glorified bodies which we are to have at the Resurrection will not be born anew "of the will of man, or of the will of the flesh"; but the spirit of God will breathe life into them again, when they shall have left in the Earth all the impurities of their first birth. Now, if the concupiscence attached to the ordinary mode of generation has thus deeply contaminated our bodies, we may be sure that the fruit of *virginal* flesh will, contrariwise, draw marvellous purity from its incorrupt root; and as Our Saviour's sacred flesh must of necessity exceed the very Sun itself in purity, He chose from eternity—as we have also seen in speaking of her conception—a Virgin Mother from whom He should take this flesh, so that she might bear her Son by faith alone, untouched by concupiscence.

What, then, must we believe this Child born to-day will become? "*Quis, putas, puer iste erit?*" To love God, and to be loved by Him, are two purely gratuitous, *supernatural*, gifts to all ordinary beings. But she is to be the Mother of God: her Divine Saviour is to be her Son. Therefore, as a mother, she will *naturally* love her Son; whilst she will have a *right* to His love, as her Child, which no other human being can possess.

From this necessary mutual love spring two important consequences. First, the greatness of the gifts that Our Lord will undoubtedly bestow on His Mother; secondly, the wonderful relation of Mary to the Eternal Father which this beautiful tie between

Mother and Child will produce :—for can the Father help loving what the Son loves ? Is it not in the very person of God the Son that heaven and earth are to be reconciled ; and are not · all our hopes actually founded on His being the eternal bond between God and man ? So that it must be taken as indisputably established that she, through whom this bond is formed, will be especially loved.

But the union of Mary with God the Father, caused by her wonderful maternity, is not merely a tie *on the human side*, as may possibly be supposed. It includes a further and peculiar privilege, the nature of which I shall now go on to discuss separately.

2.

The line of reasoning that I shall take upon this point—an exceedingly delicate one, on account of the ease with which one may fall into error on the subject —has been to some extent suggested by what has been already said of the Blessed Virgin's love for her Son. The doctrine I would now set forth rests on the conclusion that this love of hers did not stop short at His humanity ; but, taking that humanity for a connecting link, *passed on to the Divine Nature*, which is inseparable from it. If we would illustrate such a deep theological point by something familiar, we can only remember once more how the love of any really devoted mother extends to everything connected with her son :—to his friends—his general concerns—his

On the Nativity of the Blessed Virgin. 61

possessions, and so on :—but, most of all, to whatever has to do with *his own person*, about which she is apt to be sensitive to the very highest degree.

Now, let us ask, what was the Divine Nature to the Son of Mary? In what way, and how nearly, did it touch His Person? We need only our Faith to give an answer. Every day, when we say our Creed, we profess belief in " Jesus Christ—the Son of God—born of the Virgin Mary". Do we, then, understand that He whom we acknowledge as the Son of Almighty God, and He who was born of the Virgin, are two persons? Most certainly not. It is the same Person Who, being God and man, is Son of God according to the Divine Nature, and Son of Mary according to humanity. Hence it is that the Fathers declared the Blessed Virgin to be the Mother of God. It was faith in this truth that triumphed over the blasphemies of Nestorius, and that will make the devils tremble to the end of the world. Now, surely, if I say that Mary must love her Son *entirely* no one will venture to dispute it: and if it is true that *both* these natures belong to Him, then she must necessarily cherish Him as a *God-man*. The mystery of such a love, it is true, can be compared to nothing on earth ; and hence we are compelled to raise our thoughts even as high as the Eternal Father Himself to find a comparison.

Ever since human nature was joined to the Person of the Word, it has necessarily been an object of complacency to the Father. These are lofty thoughts,

I acknowledge; but, as they are really fundamental principles of Christianity, it is of importance that they should be understood by the faithful; and I shall put forward nothing that cannot be proved from the Scriptures. Of whom, then, are we to suppose that the Eternal Father was speaking when that miraculous voice from God broke forth on Mount Tabor: "This is my beloved Son, in Whom I am well pleased"?[1] Was it not of that Word made flesh who was then appearing transfigured before the eyes of His Apostles? By such an authentic declaration as this, therefore, God made it clear that His Fatherly Love reaches to the humanity of His Son; and that, having joined the human nature so closely to the Divine, He will never more separate them in His affections. In this declaration, too, if we can but thoroughly grasp it, we shall find the whole foundation of our hope to consist; for it puts before us the fact that Jesus, Who is man *even as we are*, is recognised and loved by God as His own Son.

Now, let none take scandal when I say that there is a certain likeness to this love of the Father in the Blessed Virgin's affection, inasmuch as her love embraces at once the Divinity and humanity of her Son which God's almighty Hand has so closely joined:— for God, in His mysterious counsels, having judged it fitting to decree that the Virgin should beget, *in Time*, that One Whom He is continually begetting

[1] Matt. xvii. 5.

On the Nativity of the Blessed Virgin. 63

in Eternity, has thus in some sort *associated her* with His eternal act of generation. Consider this deep mystery well: understand that to make *her* mother of that self-same Son to Whom *He* is Father, is indeed to let her take part in His own begetting. Hence, having once given her, as it were, this share in His eternal act of generation, it was becoming, and worthy of His wisdom, that a spark of His Infinite Love for that Son should enkindle her breast. As the providence of God disposes of all things with wonderful justice, it seems even necessary that He should fill the Blessed Virgin's heart with an affection far beyond that of mere nature, and reaching even to the very highest degree of grace; so that she might have for her Son feelings that should be at the same time fit for a mother of God, and worthy of a God-man. Not even the intellect of the sublimest of angels could enable one to comprehend this most perfect union of the Eternal Father with her. God "so loved the world," as Our Lord Himself says, "as to give His only-begotten Son";[1] and the Apostle further declares that He has "also, with Him, given us all things".[2]

If, then, He did this out of the true affection He had for us *because* He had given us His Only-Begotten as Master and Saviour, what far greater designs must not His unspeakable love have made Him form for Mary, concerning whom He had decreed that Jesus

[1] John iii. 16.   [2] Rom. viii. 32.

should belong to her in the same capacity in which He belongs to Him :—that she should be the Mother of His only Son, and that He would be the Father of hers?

O prodigious abyss of love! The mind gets beyond its depth in trying to think of this mysterious union: in considering what an object of delight Mary must have been to the Father, from the moment when a Divine Son—common to a woman of flesh and to the Godhead Himself—became the bond between Him and her.

Truly, then, whatever praises we may offer to a Child with this destiny are far below her deserts. The mere contemplation of her grandeur as predestined Mother of God dazzles our mental sight, and makes us unable to speak of her as we would. But, having treated of her to the best of my power in this great position, which seems to raise her so far above us, I would now bring her shortly before you in that relation to ourselves which I have referred to as a special consequence of her alliance with the Eternal Father. I may, as my final point, show how her greatness must necessarily be a beneficent greatness, and how her wonderful dignity carries with it the office of Mother of the Faithful.

3.

It is the very nature of God, who possesses in Himself every perfection and everything that can possibly have existence—every grace and gift, every beauty that we behold in creation—to *give*. One of the noblest and most worthy of many ideas that we may form of the Divine Essence is to look upon It as not only a treasure-house of unlimited perfections, but as one that must open and pour itself forth on creatures. And why? Chiefly because one of its chief attributes is *goodness*. To begin with, creatures would never exist at all if God did not draw them forth from their nothingness by imparting to them, so to speak, a share of His own Being; and we have already discussed the great extent to which His love for man makes Him go in bestowing favours upon Him. St. Augustine says that there are only three reasons for giving at all: first, *necessity*, or compulsion; secondly, *self-interest*, or expectation of some advantage in return; thirdly, *beneficence*, which proceeds from pure goodness. It is very clear that God cannot give from either of the two first motives; hence He must give out of simple *love*, which is the quality proper to goodness.

But if love is proper to goodness, fertility is proper to love. Indeed, one sort of fertility *is* love, as opposed to the fertility of nature. In the ordinary course of things we see people without children adopt them; and hence St. Augustine often calls charity "a Mother": *Charitas Mater est.*[1] Now, this double kind of fertility that we see in creatures emanates

[1] In *Ep. Joan.*, tract ii., n. 4, tom. iii., part ii., col. 838.

from the same quality in God, whence all paternity proceeds. The *Nature* of God is fruitful, and produces His Son by Nature Whom He begets in Eternity. The *love* of God is fruitful, giving Him adopted sons; and all who are His "children by adoption" are born of this second fertility. Mary shares in the natural fertility of God by begetting His own son; but as the sole cause of her dignity, and of Christ's Incarnation, is the love of God for man, she must necessarily also share in the fertility of His Love by begetting the Faithful, in whose birth she has "co-operated by her charity": *cooperata est charitate.*[1]

Mary, then, is at the same time Mother of Christ and our Mother; and this gives us double reason for keeping the anniversary of her birth with joy, since it gives her a twofold power of intercession. To be a perfectly efficacious intercessor before the throne of God, the one who pleads must possess equal nearness to God and to man; and of what creature but Mary can this be said? As Mother of Christ she is close to the Eternal Father, and as Mother of the Faithful she is close to us: hence her position as a pleader is quite exceptional.

But if she is, by virtue of her dignity and office, necessarily Mother of the Faithful, not all the Faithful are her worthy children whom she will acknowledge and help:—on certain conditions only may we rely on

[1] *St. Aug. de Sancta Virginit.*, n. 6, tom. vi., col. 343.

On the Nativity of the Blessed Virgin. 67

her powerful intercession. These conditions, however, may all be reduced to one: to the fulfilment of the Will of God after the pattern of Our Lord Jesus Christ. If Mary's existence is bound up, as we have seen that it is, in that of her Son, those only who love Him can be loved by her; and He Himself has placed the true test of love for all Christians in obedience. But our obedience is to be *like His*:—and what was that? It was very simple: Christ *pleased not Himself*.[1] He did only the Will of His Father without any choice as to what It should be; and as the Father's Will was suffering, He suffered "unto death". His Mother did the same: she had not even a sight of the glory on Mount Tabor, but had to bear her full share of the ignominy of the Cross. Nay, it was actually at the foot of the Cross that her Son specially proclaimed her our Mother; and this for two reasons:—that she might have a true experience of the deepest sorrows of motherhood, so as to sympathise with us; and that we might know how only through courageously and lovingly suffering what God wills, and taking up our cross as He has commanded, can we ever be her genuine children. And—to finish my subject with a suggestion far above ordinary human ideas—this is not all. We may do *more* than be worthy and trustful children of Mary, by doing the Will of God in all things and loving the Cross. We may even—O wonderful thought!—share in some sort the glorious privilege

---

[1] Rom. xv. 3.

of her Maternity. If this sounds impossible or presumptuous, listen to Christ Himself; for does He not say: " He who doth the Will of My Father Who is in Heaven, the same is My brother, and My sister, *and My Mother* " ?[1]

[1] Mark iii. 32, *seq.*

V.

FOR THE FEAST OF THE ANNUNCIATION.

"Creavit Dominus novum super terram: fæmina circumdabit virum" (Jerem. xxxi. 22).

OUT of that great and terrible wreck, in which human reason lost its chief possessions, and especially the Truth for which God had formed it, the mind of man has retained a vague and uneasy desire to recover some vestiges of that truth; and of this desire has been born an almost incredible love of novelty, which appears in the world in various forms, and exercises minds of various kinds. Some, it merely impels to collect countless foreign curiosities; more energetic spirits are driven by the feeling to exhaust themselves in attempts to discover fresh walks in art, or in the management of business; whilst others, again, search nature for her hidden secrets from the same motive. In short, it may be asserted of this desire for "something new" that throughout the universe no feeling has a stronger hold on human nature, or is a more common incentive to all forms of activity. To cure this disease, God Himself sets before us in Scripture what we may call, in all reverence, *holy novelties* and *profitable curiosities;* and of this to-day's Mystery is a striking instance. The Prophet has drawn our attention to it as an extraordinary and astonishing " new thing," in the words of the text ; and we are now to consider it. We must not, however, fail first to beg the help of Our Lord through His Mother by greeting her, on this day when it was first uttered, with Gabriel's salutation of *Ave !*

To find true lowliness even amongst men, amid the universal eagerness to be great in all people and at all times, is exceedingly rare. But if it is a spectacle that always strikes us afresh to see *men* remaining content with a naturally low station, it is a far more wonderfully new thing to see *a God,* stripping Himself of His supreme greatness, come down from the height of His throne and voluntarily annihilate Himself. Yet this *is* the marvel that the Church presents to our notice in the Mystery of the Word made Flesh, and which made the prophet say that " God hath created a new thing upon the earth," when He sent His Son there, humiliated and brought to nought.

Now, in this self-abasement of the God-man, there are two most extraordinary things to be noted. God is the Lord of lords, and cannot possibly behold anything above Him : God is alone in greatness, and can find none around to be His equals. Yet—O ever-new prodigy !—He Who has nothing above Him

For the Feast of the Annunciation. 71

becomes subject and gives Himself a Master; He Who is without an equal becomes man and gives Himself fellows. That Son, equal in Eternity to the Father, undertakes to become His Father's servant: that Son, raised infinitely above man, puts Himself on an equality with all men. Well, indeed, may the Prophet declare that the Creator has done *a new thing*: for never before has God had such a subject, or man such a companion. But in reflecting on this new wonder the second part of the text must be kept in mind: *fæmina circumdabit virum*. These words bring out Mary's part in this marvellous work; and we may truly express her share in it by saying that God the Son, in making Himself a subject, chose her as the *Temple* in which He would pay homage to the Father; and, in uniting Himself to men, made her the *channel* of His intercourse with them. Thus, she is associated with both sides of our subject: for Christ has honoured her by annihilating and subjecting Himself *in her*, and by communicating with man *through her*.

I.

It is a surprising but indisputable truth that, amongst the infinite means that God possesses for establishing His glory, the most efficacious of all is necessarily joined to lowliness. He may reverse the whole order of nature, or display His power to mankind by countless fresh miracles; but, marvellous as it may appear, He can never show His greatness so plainly as when He stoops to humble Himself. Here is a thing which seems strange, indeed, and new! The thought may be difficult to grasp; but the mystery we are dealing with affords plain evidence of its truth. St. Thomas[1] has clearly proved that the greatest work of God was that of uniting Himself personally to the creature, as He did in the Incarnation; and it is not nearly well enough understood that, in the whole range of unlimited possibilities, omnipotence could have found nothing more noble to do than to give the world *a God-man.* "O Lord, *Thy work!*" the prophet says[2]:—fearing not to assert that God can do nothing more wonderful.

But if it is His greatest work it is also, consequently, His greatest glory, for God is glorified only in His works: *lætabitur Dominus in operibus suis.*[3] Now, God could not work this stupendous miracle except by lowering Himself, according to St. Paul[4]:—"But debased Himself, taking the form of a servant". We must, then, echo the Prophet's words, and acknowledge that God has wrought something fresh upon earth:—and what? He chose to carry His greatness to its very highest pitch, and for this He stooped: He chose to exhibit His glory in its most brilliant light, and for this He put on our weakness. He "dwelt amongst us, and we saw His glory".[5] His

---

[1] Part. iii., quæst. i., part. 1.   [2] Habac. iii. 2.
[3] Ps. ciii. 31.   [4] Phil. ii. 7.   [5] John i. 14.

For the Feast of the Annunciation. 73

glory then showed greatest when it corresponded to the depth of His abasement.

It is not, however, merely as a "new thing," or an object of even holy curiosity, that I am dwelling on this subject. My great aim is to promote the love of that fundamental Christian virtue—*humility ;* and this, by showing God's own love for it. He cannot possibly find humility in Himself, the height of His supremacy not allowing of His abasement as long as He remains in His own nature: He must always act as God' and hence always be great. Therefore, what He cannot find in Himself he seeks in a nature that is foreign to Him. Why should this infinitely abounding Nature be willing to borrow? That He may be *enriched by humility,* which is what the Son of God came into this world to seek. He was made man in order that His Father might behold in His person *a God subject to obedience.*

That this was indeed His purpose we can see for ourselves, in Holy Scripture's words about the first thing He did on entering the world at His sacred Incarnation. St. Paul, in the Epistle to the Hebrews, shows that the first act, the first thought, and the first movement in the will of the God-man, constituted an act of obedience. Here are the Apostle's words :—
" Wherefore, when He cometh into the world ":— observe, "when He cometh ":—*ingrediens :*—" He saith : sacrifice and oblation Thou wouldest not ; . . . Holocausts for sin did not please Thee. Then said

I, behold I come": and why? Because: "in the head of the book it is written of Me that I should do Thy will, O God".[1] Here we are told in formal terms that the first act of the Son of God is one of submission and humility: *Ecce venio, ut faciam, Deus, voluntatem tuam.*

Looking further into the matter we shall find a second instance of His love for humility in that choice of the Blessed Virgin, above referred to, as the Temple wherein to offer His first vows of obedience to His heavenly Father. We shall see that the Word Who had so deeply abased and humbled Himself chose, on taking flesh, to inhabit only a dwelling that was *prepared for Him by humility.* Here, again, Scripture declares the fact; for what does it say of Mary's interview with the angel who announced the great miracle to her? It records only two sayings of hers; and, of these, one guards her chastity and the other expresses her deep humility. The beauty and significance of the first of these sayings has been dwelt upon in treating of Mary's Conception;[2] but her exquisite virginal purity did not suffice, *alone,* to prepare the Temple into which the Most High was to descend: something more was needed.

Gabriel replies to her doubt by declaring the marvellous privilege that is to be hers: "The Holy Ghost

---

[1] Hebr. x. 5, 6, 7.
[2] *Vide* Sermon i. on the "Grounds of Devotion".

For the Feast of the Annunciation. 75

shall come upon thee, and the power of the Most High shall overshadow thee".[1] And what follows? Certainly the most wonderful instance of humility and self-repression that the world has ever seen; for Mary is not for one moment carried away by either joy or elation at the mysterious dignity conferred upon her. She utters not one word beyond a simple enunciation of her submission to the Will of God. "Behold the handmaid of the Lord. Be it done unto me according to Thy word."[2] Then, at once, the Heavens are opened:— the Son of the Most High, begotten by Him from all Eternity, is conceived in the Virgin's Womb:— and this great miracle is possible because that Virgin's humility has made her capable of receiving "Him whom the Heavens cannot contain"— Immensity Itself.

With this truth before us, need we wonder if God seems far off from man, or slow to bestow His graces? For lowly hearts are hard to find on earth; and not even the sight of a God Who has taken on Him the form of a servant—who has actually made Himself nought for us—seems able to bring down our pride. Yet, if we would but learn to realise the extraordinary *grandeur* of God as shown in the utter abasement of the Incarnation, we should long to share in Mary's true glory by acknowledging the absolute nothingness whence we come, and bringing Him down into our hearts by our genuine humility.

[1] Luke i. 35.   [2] *Ibid.*, 38.

2.

But if Mary's deep lowliness, which makes her humble herself the more because of her great dignity, confers on her the glory of becoming the chosen habitation of her Maker in His own humiliation, it is still not her only greatness. God chooses her also as the means of giving Himself to man: a second "new thing" not less surprising than the first. Having considered the wonder of the voluntary subjection of a Supreme Ruler, we must now behold the One Sole and Incomparable Being taking to Himself companions and associating with men, which is to-day's Mystery. To understand this new marvel we must try to conceive a vivid idea of that perfect *unity* of God which makes Him infinite, incommunicable, and singular, in His whole being. He is the only Wise One, the only Blessed One; King of kings, Lord of lords; alone in His Majesty, inaccessible on His throne, to be compared with none in power. Man has no language strong enough fitly to express this unity; but some words of Tertullian's perhaps give as true an idea of it as is possible to human weakness. He calls God "the Supreme Great One": *Summum Magnum;* but says that " He is supreme only because He surpasses every-
" thing else; and thus, suffering naught that is His
" equal, leaves so far behind all that might be com-

"pared to Him that He makes a solitude for Himself "out of His singular excellence".[1]

If this seems a strange way of speaking, it is because Tertullian, used to strong language, seeks for new terms by which to describe a quite unexampled greatness. What can be more majestic or grand than the solitude of God? We can only conceive of It as self-contained, hidden within Its own light, separated from all things by Its own immensity: unlike all human grandeur— in which there is always some weakness or a low side as well as a high one—being equally strong and inaccessible on all sides. What a marvellous sight, then, to see this solitary and Incomparable One come forth from His august loneliness to adopt companions; and these companions, sinful mortals:—for " nowhere doth " He take hold of angels":[2] *non angelos apprehendit.* He did not stop short at the angels, though they may be called the beings nearest to Him. He strode as a giant : "leaping upon the mountains,"[3] says Holy Writ: that is, passing by the angelic choirs. He sought out human nature—relegated by the mere fact of its mortality to the lowest rank in the universe, and which had added the estrangement of sin to inequality of condition :—laid hold of it, and united it to Himself, soul and body. He made Himself a flesh like unto

---

[1] "Summum victoria sua constat. Atque ex defectione œmuli solitudinem quandam de singularitate præstantiæ suæ possidens, unicum est."—Advers. Marcion, lib. i., n. 3.

[2] Hebr. ii. 16.   [3] Cant. ii. 8.

ours. In short, God, who became man "that we also might have fellowship with Him,"[1] treated with us as with His equals, on purpose that we might be able to treat with Him as with *our* equal: *Ex æquo agebat Deus cum homine, ut homo agere ex æquo cum Deo posset.*[2] Well may we say: "For what other nation is there so great, or that hath Gods so nigh them, as our God is present to our petitions?"[3]

Much more time might be given to considering this wondrous act of condescension, if the Mystery of to-day did not make it fitting to turn our attention specially to Mary's share in it. If the Incarnation bestows an enormous benefit on our human nature, what is not the Blessed Virgin's glory in being made the means of Christ's union with that nature? He enters this world through her, and makes her the link of His blessed fellowship with us. Further, having chosen her for such a ministry, He sends one of His highest angels as His spokesman to her, as if to ask her consent. The secret of this great mystery may be found in the Order of God's Decrees, as He Himself has revealed them to us.

Scripture, and the unanimous consent of all ages, teaches that in the adorable mystery of our redemption it had always been determined by Divine Providence to use for our salvation all that had been used for our ruin. The reasons for this are too long to be entered

---

[1] John i. 3, 6.   [2] Tertull., advers. Marcion, lib. ii., n. 27.
[3] Deut. iv. 7.

For the Feast of the Annunciation. 79

upon here; it must be enough for me to say, in a word, that God chose to destroy our enemy by turning his plots back on his own head, and letting his own weapons—so to speak—be the undoing of him.

Hence, Faith teaches us that if we were lost through a man, we are also saved by one. Death reigns in Adam's race, and life is born of the same race; God uses as the remedy for our sin that very Death which was its punishment; the Tree both kills and cures us; and we see in the Holy Eucharist that a saving act of eating repairs the evil wrought by a rash act of the same kind. According to this wonderful dispensation, so clearly traceable throughout the work of our salvation, it is necessary that as both sexes took part in the ruin of our nature, both should concur in its deliverance. Tertullian taught this in the earliest centuries, in the book on *The Flesh of Jesus Christ.* Speaking of the Blessed Virgin, he says that "what had been lost by this sex must be restored by the same sex".[1] St. Irenaeus the Martyr[2] said the same before him, and St. Augustine[3] after him; and all the holy Fathers have agreed in teaching the same doctrine. Therefore the conclusion is clear that it was undoubtedly fitting for God to predestine a new Eve as well as a new Adam; so as to bestow upon earth, in place of the old condemned race, a new posterity to be sanctified by grace.

[1] *De Carn. Chr.*, n. 17. [2] *Contr. Hæres.*, lib. v., cap. xix., p. 316.
[3] *De Symb. ad Catech.*, Serm. iii., cap. iv., tom. vi., col. 571.

And certainly, if we ponder in our heart the unsearchable decrees of Providence concerning the rehabilitation of our nature, and carefully compare Eve with Mary, this old and sacred doctrine will come out with convincing clearness. I will but shortly quote here the words used by the Fathers in showing the correspondence between them.

The work of our corruption began in Eve, the work of our restoration in Mary; the word of Death was carried to Eve, the word of Life to Mary; Eve was still a virgin, and Mary is a virgin; Eve, whilst yet a virgin, had her spouse, and the "Virgin of virgins" has also hers. A curse was pronounced on Eve, a blessing on Mary:—*Benedicta tu*.[1] An angel of darkness accosts Eve, an angel of light speaks to Mary. The angel of darkness offers to raise Eve to false greatness, by making her aim at divinity:—"You shall be," he declares, "as Gods".[2] The angel of light places Mary in a state of true greatness by a holy union with God:— "The Lord is with thee," Gabriel says to her.[3] The angel of darkness, speaking to Eve, inspires her with a plan of rebellion:—"Why hath God commanded you that you should not eat of every tree of Paradise?"[4] The angel of light, speaking to Mary, persuades her to obedience:—"Fear not, Mary": and "no word shall be impossible with God".[5] Eve believed the serpent, and Mary the angel. "Thus," says

---

[1] Luke i. 42.   [2] Gen. iii. 5.   [3] Luke i. 28.
[4] Gen. iii. 1.   [5] Luke i. 30, 37.

Tertullian,[1] "an act of devout faith blotted out a fault of rash credulity, and Mary repaired, by believing in God, what Eve had destroyed by believing in the devil."

Then, to complete the mystery, Eve—seduced by the evil one—is compelled to flee before the face of God; whilst Mary—taught by the angel—is made worthy to bear her God. Eve having presented us with the fruit of death, Mary presents us with the fruit of life, in order—says St. Irenaeus[2]—" that the Virgin Mary might be the advocate of the virgin Eve".[3]

So exact a correspondence is no mere invention of the human intellect. It makes one unable to doubt that Mary is the most blessed Eve of the new Covenant, having the same share in our salvation that Eve had in our destruction—that is, the share next to that of Jesus Christ :—Mother of all the living, as Eve was of all mortals. The wonderful order of God's own designs—the fittingness of things so clearly set forth —the necessary connection of all His mysteries with each other—alike convince us of its positive truth.

And yet the brethren who have left us cannot bear us to believe that Mary is, after Jesus Christ, the prin-

---

[1] *De Carne Christi*, n. 17.

[2] *Cont. Hæres.*, lib. v., cap. xix., p. 316.

[3] These comparisons of Mary with Eve, and the language of the Fathers on the subject, is gone into very fully in chapter x. of Dr. Ullathorne's book, cited in *Note* on Conception Sermon. Perhaps the whole doctrine could hardly be more fully and tersely expressed than by the rhyme of an old English mystery play :—

" Man for Man, Tree for Tree,
Maid for Maid—so shall it be ! "

cipal co-operator in our salvation! What, then, will they do if they destroy this connection between the mysteries of God? How will they account for His sending His angel to her? Surely, He *could* have done His work in her without gaining her consent, if it had not clearly been in the Counsel of the Father that she should co-operate in our salvation and her Son's Incarnation, by her obedience and charity? Is it likely, either, that when her motherly love was so much concerned in our happiness through the Mystery of the Incarnation, that love should have now become barren, and ceased working for us?

If there are any here present who have broken with us, let me ask them whether they have left the Communion within which their fathers lived and died in the Love of Christ, because they hold us guilty of a crime for begging the help of Mary? If so, we can only reply that the whole Church Catholic will never cease to say: *Ad te clamamus, exules filii Hevae!* for she who has been pronounced, by the earliest doctrine of the Fathers, to be the advocate of Eve herself, must certainly always remain the helper of Eve's posterity:— *Advocata nostra;* and from her who was appointed to counteract the poison of that deadly fruit given to us by our first Mother, we shall always continue to ask and to receive the fruit of life :—" The blessed fruit of her womb ":—*Jesus*, Who through her has become our brother and fellow-man as well as our God, that from Him we may learn to live divinely.

VI.

ON THE FEAST OF THE VISITATION.

"Intravit in domum Zachariæ, et salutavit Elizabeth"
(St. Luke i. 40).

THE events of to-day's mystery bring before the faithful in a peculiar manner the fact that our God is *a hidden God*, and that His power works in the soul in a secret and impenetrable manner. Four people are concerned in the occurrence we are celebrating: Jesus and Mary; St. John, and his mother St. Elizabeth. Now, it is most remarkable that of all these sacred personages the only one who seems to perform no particular action is the Son of God Himself. Elizabeth, enlightened from on high, acknowledges the Blessed Virgin's dignity and humbles herself deeply before her: "Whence is this to me?"[1] John, even within Elizabeth's womb, feels his Divine Master's presence, and shows his joy in a wonderful way: he "leaped for joy".[2] Mary, marvelling at the great effects of Divine Omnipotence in herself, exalts the holy name of God and declares His munificence in her

---

[1] Luke i. 48.   [2] *Ibid.*, 44.

behalf, with her whole heart. But all this time Jesus Himself, hidden beneath His Mother's breast, gives no sensible sign of His presence. He, who is the cause of the whole mystery, takes no active part in it.

Strange as this may seem, it is not really surprising. Our Lord here hides His power intentionally, to show us how He is the invisible force that moves all things without moving Himself, and directs all things without showing His Hand. Hence, we shall find that though He may seem to be passive on this occasion His influence is fully apparent in the actions of the rest, whose movements are really all inspired by Him alone.

One of the greatest mysteries of Christianity is the holy union that the Son of God forms with us, and His secret way of visiting us. I am not speaking here of those special communications with which He now and then honours chosen souls: they must be left to the teaching of spiritual books and spiritual directors. Besides such mysterious intercourse as this, there are the visits paid by the Son of God every day to the faithful soul; interiorly by His Holy Spirit and the inspirations of grace; exteriorly by His Word, His sacraments, and above all by the Sacrament of the Most Holy Eucharist. It is of great consequence to all Christians to know what their feelings ought to be when Jesus Christ visits them; and the Gospel of to-day appears to furnish a distinct instruction on the subject. If we would thoroughly enter into its meaning, however, we must notice that whenever the Son

On the Feast of the Visitation. 85

of God comes to man He causes these successive movements to take place within him. The first thing He does is to inspire the soul with an overpowering sense of His Majesty, which fills it with awe and makes it fear and tremble at the thought of its own baseness —counting itself quite unworthy of His favours. But God cannot stop short here; for if this first feeling lasted the soul would never dare to approach Him; and therefore He causes the second movement, which consists in an intensity of *holy desires*, producing a longing in the soul to rise up and come near to its Saviour. Then, by-and-by, comes the third and most perfect operation of grace :—namely, the full answer to these ardent wishes in the complete triumph of God's own peace within the heart, as the Apostle describes it: *Pax Christi exultet in cordibus vestris.*[1] All who are deeply experienced in spiritual things know that grace makes progress in their souls by these three degrees :—that it prepares them by humility, draws them on by ardour, and at last makes them perfect by possession of that Peace of Christ which passeth all understanding.

If we study the incidents of Mary's visit to Elizabeth we shall find all these states of soul clearly represented by the characters that appear before us, and who all speak and act through the secret inspiration of Jesus.

First, then, for the Christian soul to feel a humble movement of real abasement when her Creator visits

[1] Coloss. iii. 15.

her—to offer Him the tribute of acknowledging her own littleness—is but just and right. This is why the first thing that God does when He comes to us by grace is to put into our hearts a feeling of religious fear that makes us, as it were, draw back from Him at the mere thought of how little we are worth. Thus, we read in St. Luke's Gospel that St. Peter had no sooner recognised the Divinity of Jesus Christ, by His miraculous works, than he threw himself then and there at His feet and cried: "Depart from me, for I am a sinful man, O Lord!"[1] So, again, that devout centurion whom Jesus wished to honour by a visit, being taken by surprise at such goodness could only express his feelings by acknowledging himself unworthy: *Domine non sum dignus.*[2] And what do we find corresponding to these feelings in the passage of Scripture that we have specially to study now? We learn that at the very first sight of Mary, and the first sound of her voice, her cousin Elizabeth—having learnt the holy maiden's dignity, and seeing by faith the God Whom she bears within her—is filled with astonishment and confusion, and cries out "whence is this to me, that the Mother of my Lord should come to me?"

Now, we ought to engrave the example of humility and respect given by these words of Elizabeth deeply on our own hearts; and we can only do this by trying to enter thoroughly into the motives that compelled

---

[1] Luke v. 8.   [2] Matt. viii. 8.

On the Feast of the Visitation. 87

her to humble herself in this way. Examining the words carefully, and reflecting on them, we find two separate thoughts underlying them : one thought concerning what Elizabeth already knew, and one concerning something she did not know. She saw that the Mother of her Lord had come to visit her—she recognised in her the one "blessed among women," as she herself was shortly to proclaim—and keenly felt the great honour done to her, and the impossibility of sufficiently acknowledging such an act of courtesy and friendship from one so great as Mary; and so the words *Mater Domini mei* explain her first motive for humbling herself profoundly before her young cousin. But if Elizabeth was fully alive to the honour bestowed on her by this visit, she was perfectly ignorant of its *cause ;* and herein lay the second ground of her self-abasement, for she could see absolutely nothing in herself worthy of such a favour. That the Blessed Virgin had hastened over the hill-country to see her was a fact ; but *why* she should have taken the journey at such a moment for the sake of one who could think of no claim on her condescension was an overpowering mystery to Zachary's holy wife, and she could only express the wonder it caused her by saying : *unde hoc ?*—whence could such an entirely gratuitous act of condescension proceed ? Not understanding it, all she could do was to make an offering to Christ, as He came to her with Mary, of a humbled heart with a confession of her inability to do more.

In short, all St. Elizabeth's thought, on an occasion that might well have caused self-complacency in a heart that contained the least vanity or pride, was that first she possessed nothing by which she could make due return for the honour thus shown to her, and that secondly she in nowise deserved it. And what other motives than these can any of us have for serving our God in fear, and rejoicing with trembling in His presence? For who so poor and who so unworthy as we, from both our natural condition and our own sins? Therefore, when God deigns to look upon us, we can but learn from Elizabeth how to reverence His supreme greatness by fully recognising our own nothingness, and to acknowledge His benefits by confessing our unworthiness.

There is another thought that will greatly help to make this feeling a reality and not a mere matter of words. When men receive favours from one another, no matter how great an inequality there may be between the one who confers and the one who receives a benefit or honour, nevertheless both are but creatures; and consequently the higher of the two, be he great as he may, must have *some* limit to his greatness which prevents his superiority from being absolute, because it is common to both: for what creature is without limitations? Hence no human being, conferring honours on a fellow-man, can feel that the recipient of his favours is so utterly beneath him as to have no claim whatever on his condescen-

On the Feast of the Visitation. 89

sion. But not so with God. Between Him and His creatures there can be absolutely no equality. He is solitary and supreme in greatness: the only Being to whom we can say: "Lord, who is like to Thee?[1] Glorious in holiness, terrible and praiseworthy, doing wonders";[2] the only One Who is singular and unapproachable in all things. If, then, He is so majestically great, woe be to those who vain-gloriously lift their proud heads before Him; for He will put such mighty ones down from their seat. But blessed be the humble souls who cry with the prophet, when they feel the touch of grace, "What is man that Thou art mindful of him, or the son of man that Thou visitest Him?"[3] Because they hide themselves, His face shall enlighten them; because they draw back through reverence, He will seek them out; because they fall at His feet, His Spirit of Peace shall rest upon them.

Once more:—the visit that so honoured and overwhelmed Elizabeth had not been sought by her: part of the very honour consisted in the fact that Mary had paid it of her own accord, and had thus forestalled her cousin in respect. Wonderful to relate, our God treats us, His poor creatures, in the same way. Whether the sinner who needs converting, or the just who is called to a higher life and the way of perfection, be concerned, He alike comes without waiting for us to ask Him. We are often not thinking of Him speci-

[1] Ps. xxxiv. 10. [2] Exod. xv. 2. [3] Ps. viii. 5.

ally at all—we may have even actually forgotten Him ; but He *seeks us out*—goes before us—or, as sacred language has it, "prevents" us : we feel and know His grace, suddenly present with us, as the Baptist knew it in his mother's womb, when we have done absolutely nothing to call it down.

There is, then, but one thing to be done in face of the unspeakable graciousness of the Creator :—that same thing which won the primacy of the Church for Peter, the first place as preacher for Paul, and the office of Precursor to Christ Himself for Elizabeth's son :—to humble ourselves as deeply as we know how, at sight of God's goodness and our utter unworthiness. When we have done this, and done it too with such genuine self-abasement that we feel actually *afraid* in God's presence, and inclined to draw back at His approach, there should gradually rise within us a quite other feeling. The faithful soul who has clearly seen her own lowliness goes on to experience a pure transport of longing which impels her to seek union with her God. This assertion may sound presumptuous or unreasonable, as a sequel to such thoughts of God's immeasurable distance from man as I have been uttering ; but it is true ; and we are actually bound to believe that we poor creatures may raise our desires even so high as to union with our Maker. In a former sermon I used an expression of Tertullian's to set forth in strong terms the supreme solitude and aloofness of God. I have now to dwell on His attribute

On the Feast of the Visitation. 91

of Goodness, which is just as inconceivable as His Greatness, and which brings Him near to us; and to express this I will use some words uttered by St. Gregory Nazianzen, surnamed "*the* Theologian" by the Greeks, on account of his lofty conceptions of the Divine Nature.

This great man, after calling on the whole world to desire God because of His infinite Goodness which loves to pour itself forth, and after dwelling fully on the subject, concludes thus:—" This God *longs to be longed for :* He thirsts, if you will but believe it, in the midst of His abundance. But for what does the Supreme Being thirst? It is that men may thirst for Him: *sitit sitiri.* Infinite as He is in Himself, and filled with His own riches, we can nevertheless do Him a favour—and how? By wishing Him to do us one; because He is more ready to give than others are to receive." [1]

Divine Goodness may indeed be likened to a clear-flowing stream which seems to beg of the passers-by one thing only:—to stop and drink, or cleanse and refresh themselves in its waters. In like manner the nature of God, which can never grow or lessen because of its fulness, may be said with all reverence to lack but one thing, which is that we should come and draw from It the waters of Eternal Life, whose inexhaustible source it is. Thus St. Gregory is justified in saying that our Creator thirsts for our desires, and receives

[1] *Orat.* xi., tom. i., p. 657.

as a benefit the power we bestow on Him of doing good to us.

This being so, it is insulting His bounty not to long to be the recipients of It. The transports of St. John within his mother's womb are caused by longing. He sees that his master has come to visit him, and he would fain go forth to receive Him. Holy love and ardent desires impel him to try to break his bonds by an impetuous movement. But he desires liberty for one thing only—that he may fly to his Saviour; and feels the restraint of his prison merely because it keeps him from doing so.

We have therefore good reason for invoking the holy Baptist as our helper in learning to long ardently for the Saviour of souls. He was appointed to prepare His ways, and his special ministry on earth was to make Jesus Christ be fervently desired by men. Another St. John has clearly explained this mission in his Gospel, and we should carefully attend to his words: "There was a man sent from God whose name was John: this man was not the light, but he came to bear witness of the light":—that is, of Jesus Christ, "the Light that enlighteneth every man that cometh into the world".[1] This seems a strange way of speaking: to say that St. John the Baptist, who is *not* the light, should discover to us Jesus Christ Who *is* the Light Itself. Still it is the truth—as the Gospel goes on to say in the case of Our Lord—that our

[1] John i. 8, 9.

spiritual eyes often fail to see the light that is shining brightly in our midst, until some lesser light shows it to us. St. Augustine draws out an analogy between this kind of spiritual blindness and our physical sight, which he says "takes a torch to look for the daylight":[1] that is, which is often so weak that it needs a feeble light, such as it can easily bear, to prepare it for the glare of noon : and this especially if the eye has been for a time altogether excluded from light. St. John was raised up to lead men, who had lost the light of truth, to the knowledge of Christ ; and he was to do this by acting as a torch, that should first attract them by its own lesser brightness, then make them wish for greater light, and so gradually guide them into the full blaze of day.

This being the work of the Precursor, he is to begin it from the first moment that the Master, Whose way he is to prepare, comes near him. This is why Jesus gives no sensible sign of His presence on this visit, but leaves it to be proclaimed by the miraculous movement of the unborn child at His approach. As the rising sun shows his splendour on the clouds before he appears himself, so Our Lord first calls our attention to His coming by the light and warmth He sheds on St. John, whose instant turning to the Sun of Justice as He feels His rays is intended as a call to us to rise up and go to meet our God by holy desires.

[1] In *Joan. Tract.* ii., n. 8.

The special office of St. John, then, on the great occasion of Mary's visit to his mother, is to show, by his eager response to the hidden influence of his Saviour, how the humble soul that has seen and felt the light and touch of grace should trust absolutely to the Love that has come to seek it out, and should return It by confidently forming the most ardent longings for union with its Maker. We, who have the unspeakable happiness of possessing that wondrous mode of union with Christ, the Holy Eucharist, should blush indeed at our frequent backwardness to take advantage of such a gift. How poor and feeble our desires appear by those of David! He knew his Redeemer only by expectation, but could yet cry out: "My soul hath thirsted after the strong living God—when shall I come and appear before the face of God?"[1] Would we but realise our privilege, and hunger and thirst for this Divine Food as we ought—counting nothing of value compared to our union with Jesus—He would speedily satisfy our longings by that Peace which Mary herself typifies on the Feast we are celebrating. She, indeed, must be in perfect peace; for, whilst all those who greet her arrival are but receiving the grace and call of Jesus Christ through her, she actually possesses Him. He lies beneath her heart; and the intense peace and joy that this gives her she pours forth in her glorious hymn. "My soul," she cries, on hearing Elizabeth's greeting, "doth magnify the

[1] Psalm xli.

Lord, and my spirit hath rejoiced in God my Saviour!"[1]

Now, if we study the *Magnificat* carefully, we shall find that its words throughout appear especially intended to fill our hearts with love for the Peace bestowed by God. For this marvellous Canticle first shows what is the only real principle of Divine Peace in the soul; then it goes on to declare the destruction of all things that can oppose or destroy its reign; and lastly—lest weak souls should grow discouraged or doubtful from finding the complete triumph of grace delayed till the next world—the hymn ends with the consoling reminder of God's fidelity to His promises which is to keep our hearts in peace by strengthening our trust.

Mary sets forth the true Principle of Holy Peace —its only real cause in the soul—when she tells us *why* her spirit rejoiced: "*because* He hath *regarded the humility of His handmaid*". It is because God has looked upon her, because He has deigned to cast His eyes upon His humble servant and to consider her, that she is in peace. This "look" cast upon His creature by the Creator, this showing of His Divine countenance, has indeed always been the cause of the just man's peace; and in Holy Writ God is described as looking upon His people in two separate ways: with the Look of favour and benevolence,[2] and the Look of help and

[1] Luke i. 46, 47.   [2] Psalm xxxii. 18.

protection.[1] Now Mary, who has had greater grace than any other Creature bestowed on her, and who possesses Christ in a manner that no one else can possess Him, shows by the next words of her Hymn that God has regarded *her* in both these ways; for she says that He Who is mighty has "*done great things*" in her — which is looking upon her with great favour; and that He has "*showed might in His arm*"—which is bestowing on her the Look of help and protection: that is, protection from all spiritual evil by driving away from her (as we have seen that He did in her Conception) the curses consequent on sin. Such was the manner in which God had shown His Face to the Blessed Virgin and had caused her heart to exult; and in like manner—with this doubly gracious Look—does He show It to all holy and innocent souls to whom He gives His own Peace. This is a hidden peace, as Jesus was hidden within Mary at Zachary's house: a peace that the world cannot understand, for it is driven away by its tumult to find a home in the calm and solitude of pure hearts. It is indeed impossible to describe, for it can be truly known only by experience. But wherever it may take up its abode— whether in chosen souls living a secular life, or in those within the cloister—it always has the same enemies; and those are the *false* peace and the *false* joys whose certain destruction by God Mary proclaims

[1] Psalm xxxii., 19, 20.

in the next part of her Canticle. She knows so well that the victory is to be with God in the end, that she declares—as the Just who look at God's side of things and not at the world's, always do—not that He *will* act by-and-by, but that He *has*, "scattered the proud," "put down the mighty," and "sent away the rich"; whilst He has correspondingly favoured the humble and the poor. This strange opposition between God and the World will go on as long as time shall last, and will show itself with regard to every person and thing:—what wins the favour and love of God being always the exact reverse of what pleases and satisfies the spirit of the World. But the true Children of Christ will not lose their peace of soul, nevertheless. They will despise, and even mock at, the apparent triumph of mere human ideas and worldly pomp and greatness, and will ever sing in their hearts the Canticle of God's real triumph. They will not forget that earth is but a place of exile, and the speech of its inhabitants but a foreign language to those who know where is their true Country; and hence their natural mode of expression will be the Songs of Zion, and not those of Babylon; and in the midst of tumult they will think thoughts of peace and not of affliction.

But, if their hearts should ever seem to fail them—if the time should seem long, and the universal triumph of Christ discouragingly delayed, so that their souls feel faint within them—then they will again listen to Mary and learn of her, as she closes her grand *Magnificat* with the fervent act of Faith in the Promises of her Maker: " He hath received Israel His servant, being mindful of His mercy; as He spoke to our fathers, to *Abraham and his seed for ever*".

VII.

THE HIDDENNESS AND POVERTY OF JESUS AND MARY.

(Preached on a Feast of the Purification.)

" Postquam impleti sunt dies purgationis ejus secundum legem Moysi, tulerunt illum in Jerusalem, ut sisterent cum Domino, sicut scriptum est in lege Domini " (Luke ii. 22, 23).

THE act which we call the " Purification of the Blessed Virgin " really includes under one common name three different ceremonies of the Old Law. These three ceremonies have all mysteries hidden beneath them ; and I propose to take the opportunity of the Feast for giving some explanation of these mysteries, which are very beautiful ones, and bring out certain aspects of the life of both Mary and her Divine Son in a very touching way.

Two of these ceremonies, commanded by the law of Moses, depended on the fact that women after childbirth were counted by this law to be unclean, and hence were required by God to withdraw from the Temple and from intercourse with their fellows for a time ; and after that to present themselves at the door of the tabernacle and there to purge themselves by offering a certain kind of sacrifice specially prescribed. These two ceremonies—first the retirement and then the offering—concerned the mother only, and had to be fulfilled whichever the sex of the child. The third ceremony concerned the infant. It was to be observed only in the case of men-children, and then only for the first-born.

The two first named legal regulations, then, are those that specially concern the Blessed Virgin's share in to-day's Feast. But do they really concern her? Was she in point of fact absolutely bound to fulfil them, as were other women? Obviously not. This law of the woman's withdrawal and her subsequent purificatory sacrifice implies—as is expressly shown by the wording of the enactment in Leviticus —that she had brought forth her child in the ordinary way; that is, in concupiscence. Mary, as we know, had not done this: her motherhood had sprung from Faith and Obedience alone, and she was wholly pure in it. Therefore such a law, actually, could not touch her at all. If she fulfilled it, she did so merely as it was a general rule of universal application to women after childbirth, to which there was no reason for her to be excepted, as far as appeared on the surface.

Nevertheless, had Mary so chosen, she could have obtained the exception which was really her due, from a law made for the sinful, by proclaiming the truth about herself and her Divine Son. Had she

Hiddenness and Poverty of Jesus and Mary. 101

done so she would have had every certainty of being believed, and of having her dignity as Mother of the Messias acknowledged before men. In the first place, she had the Truth to support her—always so powerful in itself when undoubtedly present; then the well-known beautiful innocence and purity of her own life, and the perfect sincerity with which everybody must have unhesitatingly credited her. Lastly, there would have been the unimpeachable testimony of such a man as Joseph to the fact that she who passed as his wife was a pure Virgin, and had borne her Child by the Power of the Holy Ghost; whilst to his own assertion he could have added the miraculous assurance of the Angel.

Yet, in spite of all, Mary made no explanation whatever. She kept absolute silence, and fulfilled the law simply, as if she were subject to sin like others; thus confirming amongst her fellows the belief that she was a married woman and had only an ordinary child. Now, this *silence* of Mary's when, obeying the Law of her People, she presented herself at the Temple, is the mystery hidden under the ceremony of her Purification; and if we consider her history as recorded in the Gospels we find that it is part of the practice she had followed ever since she had known of her own great dignity from the Angel Gabriel. She had always refrained from proclaiming her exception from ordinary rules; and, with the most wonderful modesty and self-restraint, had kept perfect silence on the subject, after just once breaking forth in her *Magnificat* to Elizabeth :—and even this, not till her cousin had spoken so as to show her own knowledge of the marvel that had happened. Others, we find, speak of her Son as what He is :—we know that the shepherds had done so at Bethlehem, and that Mary had " kept these words and pondered them in her heart "[1]—but none of hers are recorded. Now, again, Holy Simeon pours forth his feelings on beholding the longed-for Messias with fervour that might well have incited the mother who stood by to break her silence ; but she contents herself with listening, attending, meditating on what is said and cherishing it in her heart : she does not speak.

What is the reason of this wonderful silence and self-suppression in the Redeemer's Mother ? It is simply that she *is* His Mother:—that is, the Mother of Him Who, after His glorious Transfiguration, said to His disciples: "Tell the vision to no man, till the Son of Man be risen from the dead " ;[2] and Who showed, by many other sayings recorded in the Gospel, that though He deigned to feel even some actual *impatience* for the humiliations of His cross (*e.g.*, " I have a baptism wherewith I have to be baptised, and how am I straitened till it be accomplished ? "[3]) yet He never had the slightest desire for His Name to be manifested before the predestined time fixed by Divine Providence. Mary's feelings, then, were

[1] St. Luke ii. 19. [2] Matt. xvii. 9. [3] Luke xii. 50.

Hiddenness and Poverty of Jesus and Mary. 103

inspired by Him that she might plainly show herself to be animated by the same Spirit. Therefore she kept her great happiness for herself and God alone, sharing it with none but those to Whom it pleased the Holy Ghost to reveal it. She waited for her Maker to disclose the Wonder when it should be expedient for the glory of His own name. God, and Jesus her beloved Son, knew that she was a spotless Virgin :—that was enough for her.

Surely—besides the mystery of its conformity to the conduct of Jesus—we have, in this unbroken silence and reserve of Mary's, a most beautiful picture of a soul perfectly satisfied with the testimony of God and its own conscience alone. Here is she, the fully enlightened Mother of Jesus, content to be merely one of the listeners when her Only Son is the subject of discourse—not speaking even when her own Virginity seems to be in question—letting the world think exactly what it likes and what God chooses it to think—hiding her great glory and repressing all words concerning a joy that must be almost too great to bear! Here is indeed a model for all men how to make Jesus, the Hidden God, Who inspired this deep humility in His Mother, satisfy all the desires of their souls, and to seek no human sympathy or approval in their sufferings or for their actions.

The second ceremony—or, more truly, the second part of the whole ceremony—prescribed to the woman consisted in a particular kind of sacrifice that she was to offer for her cleansing. Now, different victims were allowed here, according to the circumstances of the person who offered them: as we know from the book of Leviticus.[1] The usual one was a year-old lamb, and either a pigeon or a turtle-dove; but if the woman who came for her purification was too poor to bring a lamb, then she might substitute for it a second turtle-dove or pigeon, and so make her offering of two birds only. Hence the turtle-doves or pigeons were especially the holocaust and sin-offering of *the poor*. Which of these victims, then, was sacrificed by the Mother of the King of Heaven? We find that St. Luke, in his account of Mary's purification, merely says that she came to the Temple to make a " sacrifice according as it is written in the Law of the Lord, a pair of turtle-doves, *or* two young pigeons ";[2] he does not say which, and he does not mention the lamb at all. Now, there may be a mystical reason for this last omission. The evangelist very likely means us to understand by his silence on that point that to offer a Lamb in the temple when " the Lamb of God Who taketh away the sins of the world " was brought there Himself would have been quite unsuitable. But, if this is so, there is also undoubtedly another meaning attached to the absence of precision as to the sacrifice offered by Mary in St. Luke's account; and that meaning is to call our attention most particularly to the *poverty* of Christ

[1] Lev. xii. 6, 8.   [2] Luke ii. 24.

and His holy mother. We are to understand that, whichever was the precise offering brought after Our Saviour's birth, it was certainly the offering of the poor. And this, next to the hiddenness, is the aspect of Our Lord's life—and, in union with Him, of Mary's —that the Feast of the Purification brings out so strongly. It calls us to meditate on the fact that never was there a man poorer than was the Saviour of mankind on earth. His foster-father had to earn his living by the work of his hands; and He Himself had not a place of His own whereon to lay His head. If, as has sometimes been the case in the world's history, both great and holy men have had the nature of their careers indicated at their birth by the appearance of certain marvellous signs, it may indeed be truly said that the beginning of Our Redeemer's life was an exact prognostication of His after years. The most wretched of mankind have usually at least some little miserable place they can call their own, in which their children may first see the light, whilst He was rather exposed than born in a stable, rejected even by His own People. The very sign by which the shepherds should know Him was His being laid in a manger for a cradle; and this first indication was fully carried out to the very end: for was He not even buried in a tomb not belonging to His mother, and wrapped and embalmed with linen and spices given in alms by His friends? Hence He chose that the sacrifice brought for His Mother's Purification should be in keeping with the rest, and should serve as yet another reminder to us that the King of Glory "being rich became poor, for our sakes; that through His poverty we might be rich".

We must now shortly consider the third ceremony included in the Law; and in doing this shall see that there was a further reason for the poverty of Mary's offering, in the fact that the presentation of Jesus Himself was a symbol of that very Death which was to be so utterly destitute. This third ceremony consisted in bringing every *first-born* man-child to offer him to God at the Altar, and then *redeeming* him by a certain sum of money, as a testimony that the child belonged by right to God and that the parent kept him only by a kind of special agreement.

Two reasons are given in the Book of Exodus for this regulation, but one only of these belongs strictly to the Mystery of to-day: and it is one worth considering. Almighty God, in order to show His dominion over all things, was accustomed to exact the "first-fruits" of everything as a kind of tribute and acknowledgment, by which man should testify that he holds his possessions only by his Maker's munificence. For this reason He required that all the first-born, of men and of animals, should be offered to Him as the Master of all. Hence, immediately after the words by which the consecration of the first-born is ordered—"Sanctify unto Me all the first-born . . . as well of men as of

Hiddenness and Poverty of Jesus and Mary. 107

beasts"—He adds the reason: "For they are all Mine".[1] And He exacted this tribute particularly in the case of men, that He might be recognised as the True Head of all the families in Israel; and that in the persons of the eldest sons, who represent the stem of the family, all the other children might be devoted to His service. Thus, the first-born were separated by this offering from common and secular things, and passed into the ranks of holy and consecrated ones. This is why the law is promulgated in these words: "Thou shalt *set apart* all that openeth the womb for the Lord".[2]

Tertullian has called Jesus our Saviour "the Illuminator of the Old Law," which was only established to typify the mysteries of His life; and the saying is especially applicable here, for who was ever more completely sanctified to the Lord than the Son of God Himself, Whose Mother was filled with the Power of the Holy Ghost? He was truly "the first-born of every creature,"[3] as St. Paul calls Him, and He is moreover the "first-fruits" of the whole human race. To-day, therefore, they come and offer Him to God at His holy Altar, to testify that *in Him alone* we are all sanctified and renewed, and that *through Him alone* we belong to the Eternal Father and have access to the throne of His Mercy. It was this that made Him say, in His great prayer for His disciples, "And for them do I sanctify Myself,"[4] that so the prophecy might be

[1] Exod. xiii. 2.   [2] *Ibid.*
[3] Coloss. i. 15.   [4] John xvii. 19.

fulfilled which promised our fathers that "in Him all nations should be blessed":[1] that is, sanctified and consecrated to the Divine Majesty. Such are His prerogatives as Eldest Son of the Father, and such our obligations to that devoted "first-born," our Saviour Jesus Who sacrificed Himself for love of us.

And here we may profitably call to mind the words of the thirty-ninth Psalm, which St. Paul puts into Our Lord's mouth in His Epistle to the Hebrews, which seem to apply exactly to the ceremony we are considering. St. Paul says: "Wherefore when He cometh into the world, He saith: . . . Holocausts for sin did not please Thee: then said I, Behold I come!"[2] meaning, the Apostle understands, that He came for the work of our salvation. Observe that Our Lord is described as saying these words when He first enters this world: *ingrediens in mundo*. Now, the Child Jesus was but six weeks old when they brought Him to present to God in the Temple, so that one may truly look upon Him as only just entering the world. We may therefore represent Him to ourselves as offering Himself voluntarily to the Eternal Father, at the same moment that His Mother presents Him according to the Old Law as her first-born, in place of all the ancient victims, so as to perfect us for ever by the oneness of His Sacrifice. Hence this ceremony is truly, as I said above, a preparatory symbol of His Passion: and here is the deep mystery hidden in the

[1] Gen. xxii. 18. [2] Heb. x. 6, 7.

special part borne by the Holy Infant in the great act of to-day.

And what, we may naturally wonder, were Mary's own feelings and thoughts on this mysterious presentation of her Divine Son? Undoubtedly she entered fully into the spiritual meaning of the ceremony, and united her will and intention to those of the infant Saviour Himself. Just as she had given her full and free consent on the day of the Annunciation to the Incarnation of the Messias, so we cannot doubt that she now ratified with her whole heart the covenant He made, on being offered as victim for His people, about His Passion and Death. This conviction is strengthened by Simeon's words; for the holy man, after uttering all his joy and gratitude at sight of the Messias in his *Nunc Dimittis*, turns to Mary and makes that strange and sad prophecy of the sword that is to pierce her Mother's heart. We cannot believe that he would have been inspired to do this, on an occasion that appeared outwardly to be full of nothing but joy, had it not been that, amongst the many things about her Son which Mary had to keep and ponder in her heart, was the knowledge of the bitter chalice He would have to drink as the consummation of the sacrifice begun on this day. This subject will be more fully treated in connection with another Feast; what we have to learn now is that the three mysteries concealed beneath the ceremonies of the Purification should be to us so many reminders, when we reflect on them, that the life of Mary with Jesus on earth was to be not only a hidden and a poor one, but a life full of the inward and unspoken sufferings of painful anticipation : all alike freely accepted by her with absolutely perfect conformity to the Spirit of her Son and the will of the Eternal Father.

VIII.

ON THE BLESSED VIRGIN'S COMPASSION.

(Preached on the Friday in Passion Week.) [1]

"Stabat autem juxta crucem Jesu, mater ejus" (St. John xix. 25). "Dixit Jesus Matri suæ: Mulier, ecce filius tuus, deinde dicit discipulo: Ecce Mater tua" (St. John xix. 26).

IN sacred and profane history alike, *last words*—that is, the words addressed by the dying to those they leave behind—are held to be of extreme interest, wherever recorded; and when such words are spoken to those whom the one departing has loved and been loved by most upon earth, then they come down to us invested with a double interest and importance.

Now, the two beings whom the Evangelist St. John loved best in the whole world were, first His Divine Master and then that Master's holy Mother, whilst he, in his turn, was his dear Lord's chosen friend; and hence he has taken special care to record for our benefit the last words spoken by Christ to Mary and himself. Well, indeed, were those words worth hand-

[1] That is, the Friday *before* Palm-Sunday.

ing down to posterity, and a most beautiful subject they form for meditation; for they bring before us a touching picture of Jesus Our Saviour, dying in absolute want—having throughout all His public life had nowhere to lay His head—His last garment having gone to the soldiers who cast lots for it—stripped by His executioners of almost the very semblance of humanity—and yet *bestowing* something from the midst of His abject poverty:—leaving a precious pledge of His friendship to those He loves before He departs this life. This pledge, moreover, is a double one; for He not only gives His beloved Mother to His friend, but makes over that friend to her. He gives them *both* away, and in so doing leaves them *to each other*, so that His legacy benefits both at once: " Behold thy son !" " Behold thy mother !"[1]

Now, in Our Lord's last humiliation, all His disciples had for the time being forsaken Him, but this one—his well-beloved John; hence he alone was left to stand for all the faithful at the foot of the Cross. We therefore hold that this most precious legacy left by Christ to the Evangelist was left in his person to every one of us; and that we in like manner were given, in him, to Christ's Mother. She, standing by the Cross and hearing the words: *Ecce filius tuus!* received through her Son's chosen Apostle that special office of Motherhood to all the adopted children of God—that " fertility of love "—which I have referred

[1] St. John xix. 26.

On the Blessed Virgin's Compassion.

to before as having been intentionally conferred upon her in the midst of sorrows.

Mary at the foot of the Cross, then, heroically enduring the keenest anguish that a mother could endure, with the full meaning and consequence of her presence there, is the subject we must consider to-day.

And, first, no one must suppose that Our Saviour's Mother was called to this post of anguish merely that she might have her heart torn by gazing on the horrible spectacle of her Only Son's torments. Providence had higher designs than this on her, when she was brought to the feet of Jesus abandoned. It was the Eternal Father's will that she should be not only offered in sacrifice with that innocent victim, and nailed to the Cross by the very same nails that pierced His flesh, but that she should share in the accomplishment of the whole mystery wrought by His Death. This is an important truth; and I would here lay before you as clearly as possible the foundations on which it rests.

Observe, to begin with, that three things concurred to make Our Saviour's sacrifice perfect. First, there were the sufferings that crushed and broke His humanity; then there was the humble resignation with which He submitted to His Father's Will; and lastly there was His giving birth to us, in grace, by His own death. To suffer as a Victim—to submit as making a voluntary offering—and to bring forth for God a new people, begotten of His wounds, in suffering: these were the three great acts to be consummated by the Son of God on the Cross. The sufferings concerned His humanity, which was to bear the burden and the punishment of our crimes; the submission concerned His Father Who, having been angered by disobedience, was to be appeased by obedience; whilst the begetting of children concerned us; for, the pleasure of our first and criminal father having caused our death, the sorrow of our second and innocent one must restore us to life.

In every one of these three divisions of Our Lord's great Sacrifice Mary is to have a share. For this she is called close to the Cross, to its very foot, that there the Holy Spirit may impress on her these three sacred marks, or characters, of her Son's passion, and so make of her a true and living image of Christ Crucified. Holy Simeon had prophesied that a sword should pierce her heart, and *here* she was to receive that sword's sharpest stroke: here also, by her very closeness to the instrument of our Redemption, she was to gain her strongest likeness to her Son: *Stabat juxta Crucem.*

We will consider the Blessed Virgin's part in each of Christ's sacrificial acts separately, and in the order I have named; therefore we must first contemplate her sufferings. To depict the sufferings of even an ordinary mother, truly, is no easy task; and the only possible way of bringing Mary's grief at her Son's passion before one's mind, vividly enough to realise it at all, is to recall the oft-repeated fact that the source of her martyrdom at the sight of His torments was the same as that of her joy in being His Mother— her peculiar and surpassing *love* for Him. All other martyrs have needed executioners and implements of bodily torture—the fire, the rack, the wheel, the pincers —to impress the mark of Christ on their quivering flesh. For her, none of this horrible apparatus is needed; and whoso imagines that it is can but little understand the nature of her love. One cross is enough for her and her Beloved; she endures the pangs of all *His* wounds by only gazing on them; her heart makes her torments exquisite, and ranks her at the head of martyrs, without any need for her body to be touched. If any one inclines to doubt this, let him think for a moment of the many mothers, loving their children only in the order of nature, who would confess to feeling those children's pains as if they were their own. Look at that Canaanitish woman in the Gospels at the feet of her Saviour! See her tears— hear her cries—and you will hardly be able to decide whether she herself, or her poor devil-tormented child, is suffering most. " Have mercy on me, O Son of David! my daughter is grievously troubled by a devil."[1] She says not "have pity on my *daughter*," but "have pity on *me*". Why? Because the fact of her child's terrible sufferings, she takes for granted, is enough to make *her* an object of compassion. She seems to bear her afflicted offspring once more within

[1] Matt. xv. 22.

her own body, and to be herself tormented with her: so says St. Basil of Seleucia,[1] dwelling at length on this story; and the woman here depicted is but a vivid example of what innumerable mothers are capable of feeling through mere love. If, then, the natural maternal tie alone can produce such wonderful sympathy in suffering, surely such a bond as that between Mary and her Divine Child must make *her* sorrows reach a depth far beyond description. In fact, it is no exaggeration to say that the intense feelings of the Canaanitish woman, and of all ordinary women typified by her, are but faint reflections of the Blessed Virgin's utterly unselfish anguish at the foot of the Cross.

Again, if we would attempt a right estimate of her grief, we must not only remember that it has its source in her love: we must go farther back, and reflect on the source of that love itself. It is unnecessary to say much on this subject here, as it has been dwelt on in treating of Mary's Nativity and the glories to which she was born; but it will help towards realising her sorrow to keep in mind that her love differs not only in *degree*, but in *kind*, from that of other women. We shall do this best by recalling shortly what has already been said of the origin of her motherhood:—namely, that it originated not at all in nature, but purely in grace; and was brought about by her own acts of faith and obedience. Further, we have seen that she was allowed in a mysterious way to share in the

[1] Orat. xx. in Chanau.

On the Blessed Virgin's Compassion. 117

Paternity of God the Father by being made the human mother of His only-begotten Son. Since, then, Mary's maternity has a supernatural source, her maternal love must have the same; and hence (whilst *including* all natural affection) is of a far higher kind than the love of mere nature.

The Blessed Virgin, in short, loves the Son at Whose cruel death she is assisting in something the same way—though of course in an infinitely less degree—that the Eternal Father loves the Word Who is His own Image and Substance. Such a love as this, emanating as it does from the very principle of all unity, must necessarily produce a union and a power of inter-communication, between Jesus Christ and His holy Mother, corresponding in some sort to the perfect union subsisting between God the Son and His Divine Father. Now, considering what unspeakably keen sympathy a union of this kind must engender, we are surely justified in believing that Mary's sorrow as a mother was unlike any other that ever has been or ever will be, both in itself and in its effects. The Father and the Son share the same glory in Eternity, the Mother and the Son share the same sufferings in Time :—for the Father and Son one fount of joys, for the Mother and Son one torrent of griefs; for the Father and Son a single throne, for the Mother and Son a single cross. If they pierce His head with thorns, Mary's brow is torn with every point of the sharp crown ; if they offer Him gall and vinegar to drink, Mary tastes the draught in all its bitterness; if they stretch out His body on a cross, Mary's limbs are racked by the violence. What brings all this about but her love? Surely, in such a sad case, she may cry with St. Augustine, though in another sense than his: *Pondus meum amor meus!*[1] for how heavily does not her love oppress her mother's heart! It is like a band of iron round her breast, tightening it so as to stifle her very sobs. It is as a leaden weight on her head, all the harder to bear that she cannot relieve her oppressive sadness by tears. It overwhelms her whole body with a crushing languor, till her limbs nearly fail her altogether. But the heaviest part of all her trouble is that she knows it is adding to Christ's trouble, and that she is constrained against her will to grieve Him by the sight of her own grief, to which she knows He is pitifully alive. Mother and Son see their respective sufferings reflected as in two mirrors, while they gaze each on the other, and have their pains indefinitely multiplied by this mutual reciprocity of feeling. The Blessed Virgin's love momentarily increases her anguish, because it is powerless either to console Jesus or to lessen His torments—but on the contrary is compelled to be the means of redoubling them; for it is the intimate knowledge of His Mother's intense love that makes her Son so keenly realise the intensity of her grief, and thus suffer more from the reaction on Himself.

[1] *Conf.*, lib. xiii., cap. ix., tom. i., col. 228.

On the Blessed Virgin's Compassion. 119

Still, however true and high reasons we may find for the depth of Mary's sorrows at the foot of the Cross, they must always remain really incomprehensible to us. It is better, in face of them, rather to do our best to imitate and sympathise than to try to understand what we cannot. With the week that we are about to enter upon before us, the sight of Christ's mother racked with *His* torments, and absolutely dead to everything but Him, should move us at least to desire such compassion for our Redeemer's sufferings as will make us indifferent to worldly pleasures. Well for us if we can go further, and learn that there is no lot so really blessed as that of being allowed a share in the Cross of Jesus, and receiving the gift of incessant mourning for His sufferings and our sins. If we doubt our own courage for accepting such a lot we may get help by meditating on the next point we have to consider: namely, Mary's part in the perfect submission and voluntariness of Christ's Sacrifice, which is shown by her *manner* of enduring her share in His sufferings.

Now, great afflictions may be nobly overcome in three different ways. First, by actually banishing all mourning or sadness about them, and losing even the sense of grief; secondly, by bearing them with resolute patience, though the soul be troubled by them never so sorely; thirdly, by feeling the sorrow itself with the greatest keenness, and yet not feeling any trouble or disturbance about it. In the first of these states, all feeling of sorrow has passed, and we enjoy perfect repose: "I am filled with comfort. I exceedingly abound with joy in our tribulation,"[1] says St. Paul: that is, a holy and even superabundant joy seems to have banished all sense of trouble. In the second state, we fight against our affliction with patience; but the struggle is so severe that, though the soul be victorious, it cannot possibly be peaceful. "Indeed," Tertullian declares, "the very opposite is the case :— the soul troubles and disturbs itself by its very effort to be calm; and, though not crushed down by weakness, is shaken by its own resistance and upset by force of its own firmness."[2] But in the third state— which can be reached only by a great miracle—God bestows such great strength against suffering that its full violence can be borne without the disturbance of our peace. Thus, in the first of these three states tranquillity banishes suffering; in the second, suffering prevents tranquillity; whilst the third unites the two, and joins extreme suffering to supreme tranquillity of soul.

Holy Scripture frequently compares grief to a troubled sea :—"The waters are come in even to my soul";[3] "my calamities . . . have overwhelmed me with their paths as with waves;"[4] for instance :—and Almighty God's three ways of overcoming our grief may be actually illustrated from three different means

---

[1] 2 Cor. vii. 4. [2] Tertull., *de Anima*, n. 10.
[3] Ps. lxviii. 1. [4] Job xxx. 12.

used by Our Lord to subdue the waters. At one time we see Him simply *command* the winds and waves, and then there comes, says the Evangelist, " a great calm ".[1] Even so God, when He chooses, calms a soul tossed about with troubles by simply sending forth His Holy Spirit upon that soul and bidding its tempests to cease : " our flesh had no rest . . . but God, Who comforts the humble, *comforted us* ".[2] Here is God calming the waves of the soul and restoring her lost serenity.

On another occasion Christ gives the waters their will, and lets the waves rise with furious vehemence, so that the vessel—driven violently before them—is threatened with instant shipwreck ; while Peter, struggling through the waters, expects to be buried in their depths. Nevertheless, Our Lord guides the ship and bears up the trembling Apostle with His own hands.[3] Thus a soul, struggling with very violent grief, feels as if she must be overwhelmed and swallowed up by it : " we were pressed out of measure above our strength " : [4] but Christ gives the poor soul such firm support that the tempest of sorrow, while shaking her to her very foundations, cannot lay her low. This is the second state above referred to. Now we come to the last, noblest, and most glorious way whereby Jesus mastered the waters. Again He gives full rein to the storm, and allows the winds to

[1] Matt. viii. 26.
[2] 2 Cor. vii. 5, 6.
[3] Matt. xiv. 24-32.
[4] 2 Cor. i. 8.

lash the waves into fury and make them rise to a fearful height. Then, treading the angry billows under foot, He walks firmly and confidently over them as if glorying in His power to brave the ungovernable element even in its fiercest rage.[1] In like manner does God let suffering loose upon us that it may act with its fullest force, so that we "should not trust in ourselves but in God Who raiseth the dead".[2] Then the faithful soul, strong and confident amidst this spiritual tumult, lets the waves of trouble surge harmless around her, and walks over them with so calm and even a step that they are compelled, against their very nature, to serve for her support. Here we have the third and highest supernatural way of overcoming afflictions, and the one in which Jesus Christ Himself overcomes His.

The Blessed Virgin, watching Our Saviour die, is in this third state of soul. The flood of grief rises high above her head—the storm-driven waves of sorrow dash against her heart—a very gulf of misery seems to open in the waters beneath her feet and threaten her destruction—but her constancy remains unshaken. Not for a moment does she wish for any abatement of the sufferings that make her like unto her Son, or for any comfort to help her in bearing them. She dreams not of asking the Eternal Father to lessen her anguish by one single throb, when she beholds Him pouring out the full vials of His wrath

[1] John vi. 17-21.   [2] 2 Cor. i. 9.

On the Blessed Virgin's Compassion. 123

on the head of His Only-begotten till Jesus Himself must perforce call aloud that His Father has forsaken Him. However terrible her griefs, nothing could grieve her so much as to receive treatment less severe than His, and not to feel all the pangs of Her Beloved. She *wills* that her sorrows should reach their very utmost possible limit in union with His, and that she should be able to say with Him, "all thy heights and thy billows have passed over me".[1] Let the storm of grief rage as it will, the Holy Spirit will never allow His own temple to be shaken, for He has laid "the foundations thereof in the holy mountains,"[2] and will keep it firm under every shock. The higher region of Mary's soul, in which her Heavenly Spouse has made His dwelling-place, will keep its serenity undisturbed amid the tempest.

St. John Chrysostom, commenting on to-day's Gospel, calls our attention to one particular aspect of Christ about to yield up His soul on the Cross, which will clearly show the reason of His holy Mother's attitude at the foot of that Cross if we meditate on it here. It is the marvellous *calmness* and *self-possession* of Jesus in His agony that fills this great Saint with admiring awe. On the eve of His death, the preacher bids us observe, Our Lord sweats, trembles and shudders at the terrible vision of His torture that rises before Him; but when His heavy troubles have actually come upon Him He

[1] Ps. xli. 8.   [2] Ps. lxxxvi. 1.

seems to be another man, to whom torments are indifferent. He talks quietly to the happy thief; He looks upon and recognises all those of His own people who are at the foot of the Cross, speaks to them, and comforts them; and at last—seeing that He has accomplished all He had to do, and carried out the Will of His Father in every particular—He gives up His Soul to Him in such a peaceful, free and deliberate manner that there can be no doubt of its being His own act. It is just as He had said:— "No man taketh it away from Me, but I lay it down of Myself".[1]

The holy doctor then goes on to ask the meaning of this: how it was that the fear of suffering oppressed Him so terribly, when the suffering itself hardly seems to touch Him? And he answers that the reason probably is that the scheme of our redemption was necessarily a work of strength and weakness combined. Christ wished to show by His fears that, like unto us, He felt trouble keenly; whilst by His firmness He had to prove that He could perfectly master His feelings and make them yield to His Father's Will. Such is the reason of our Redeemer's attitude at this supreme moment given by St. John Chrysostom; and doubtless it is a solid one. Yet other reasons too may be found; and I venture to suggest one in connection with the present subject which seems of even a higher kind, and to go nearer to the heart of the mystery.

[1] St. John x. 18.

On the Blessed Virgin's Compassion. 125

I think we may believe that one most probable cause of Our Lord's peace on Calvary, when the Mount of Olives had witnessed His agony, was the fact that the Cross on Mount Calvary found Him in the very act of His Sacrifice, and there is no action in the world that should be performed in so calm a spirit as this one. Those who let their thoughts wander here and there without restraint, according as curiosity or inclination suggest, while present at the Holy Sacrifice of the Mass, cannot have the least idea of what *Sacrifice* means.

Sacrifice is an act by which we offer our homage to God; and who does not know that any act of respect demands a quiet and collected demeanour? It is the very nature of respect to require this. God sees into the depth of all hearts, and holds us to be wanting in due respect for His majesty when our souls are uncontrolled and distracted in His presence. How important, then, that the High priest who actually offers the sacrifice should do so with a perfectly calm mind! The oil with which Aaron is anointed— that symbol of peace poured so abundantly over his head—is in fact intended to warn him of the peace that he should attain to in his own mind and heart by banishing every distracting thought and feeling. Hence it was, we cannot doubt, that Our Divine Pontiff Jesus Christ showed Himself so perfectly calm in His death-agony. If He had appeared troubled on Mount Olivet, it was, says St. Augustine, a *voluntary* anguish that He suffered; for only by his own will could it affect Him; and for this reason:—He was then, in His own eyes, simply the *victim*, and as a victim He willed to behave. Therefore He adopted—if we may be allowed to say so—the very actions and posture of a victim which was being dragged, terrified and shuddering, to the altar. But on the Cross it is quite otherwise. He it now at the altar, as *priest;* and from the moment that His innocent hands have been raised to present Himself as our victim to the Wrath of Heaven, He is exercising His priestly function; and He will allow no more fear to be seen lest it should imply any repugnance for the sacrifice. His Divine Will, to which all His emotions are subject, prevents the peace of His Soul from being troubled and represses all outward sign of anguish; and thus we are made to understand that our most merciful High-Priest offers Himself for us quite freely and from pure love of our salvation. According to St. Augustine, again, "He dies as gently as we might go to sleep".[1]

Now, Mary is appointed to share in this great sacrifice, and to offer up her own Son; and this is why she, as well as He, gathers up her full strength and stands composed and upright beneath the Cross. This is why, despite all her sufferings, she gives Him with her whole heart to the Eternal Father to be the victim of His vengeance. We must remember, too, that Christ's Mother did not offer up her Son on this one

[1] Tract. cxix., n. 6.

On the Blessed Virgin's Compassion. 127

occasion only: she had been offering Him unceasingly from the moment when Holy Simeon had, by God's command, foretold to her the strange contradictions of which he was to be the object, and which were to "pierce her heart with a sword".[1] She had not known *what* the contradictions were to be, nor to what special manner of persecution her beloved Son was to be subject; but she had always had to endure the double torment of knowing that He *must* suffer, and of being in uncertainty as to how: so that she herself, as Jesus grew up under her eyes, suffered His passion over and over again, in anticipation that was all the more terrible from being vague. But through it all she never slackened in her perfect submission to the Will of God; and she showed this resignation by the double act of accepting the uncertainty and of being ready to offer the Child in whatever way it should please His Father when the time and manner should be disclosed. Ever since He had lain a little infant in her arms she had looked upon Him as a Victim; and now that she sees the death-blow inflicted on the Cross she is but completing the sacrifice that she had begun to take part in long ago. Just as Our Saviour Himself takes care to show that He makes His Sacrifice voluntarily, so she would rather have her very heart torn out than withhold for a moment her full consent to His passion and death.

But she is to receive more than she has offered

[1] Luke ii. 34, 35.

up; for God will restore that well-beloved Son to her arms, and meantime He gives her for children all His Christian people. He does this, as we have seen, through the faithful Apostle who has himself described the wondrous mystery in the Apocalypse:—" And a great sign appeared in heaven : a woman clothed with the sun, and the moon under her feet, and on her head a crown of twelve stars: and being with child, she cried travailing in birth, and was in pain to be delivered ".[1] St. Augustine declares that this woman is the Blessed Virgin,[2] and there are many convincing proofs to be given for the statement. But how can the painful child-birth here named be explained, when it is the belief of the Church that Mary was exempt from the common curse of mothers, and brought forth her Son without suffering just as she conceived Him without concupiscence? These assertions seem contradictory, but are in fact not so; for the bringing forth of Jesus Christ and of the Faithful are two separate births, and this passage of Scripture is interpreted of the latter. Mary brought forth the Innocent One painlessly; but she is to become the Mother of *sinners* amidst grief and tears, the natural effect of the high price she has to pay for her universal maternity. This price is no less than her only Son, whom she must see die before she can bring forth God's adopted children, and of whom it is

---

[1] Apoc. xii. 1.
[2] Serm. iv., *de Simp. ad Catec.*, cap. i., tom. vi., col. 575.

On the Blessed Virgin's Compassion.

therefore truly said that she bore them in pain and sorrow. And in this painfully-acquired second motherhood she is again mysteriously sharing the characteristics of the Eternal Father's own Paternity; for has *He* not given up His Son by nature, and delivered Him to death, that He might make man into His Son by adoption and co-heir of His Only Begotten? By the same love with which He delivers up, forsakes, and sacrifices His Divine Son He adopts, quickens, and regenerates us: almost as though He wished to justify His adoption of us by in some sense losing His rightful Heir to make room for us. We can never sufficiently wonder at, or be grateful enough for, love such as this.

If Mary, then, is to take her part in fulfilling the third condition of Christ's perfect sacrifice, whereby He begets a new and regenerate family of children for His Divine Father *by the Cross*, the reason is clear for her being appointed Mother of the Faithful at the foot of that Cross and nowhere else. She is the Eve of the New Covenant, as we have seen; and in that capacity must make satisfaction for the sin of our first mother just as the Second Adam makes it for that of our first father. She is destined to do this by uniting her will to the Eternal Father's Will, and making *with Him* the sacrifice of the Son common to both. And how is the sacrifice carried out? By means of a few words spoken by Jesus from His bed of death that must have pierced her heart with a stab sharper than any she had felt in her whole life before. What does she hear Him say as He hangs dying before her eyes? What is His last farewell? "Woman, *behold thy son*," He says. We have but to think for a moment over these words to realise that all the pangs Mary ever suffered must have been concentrated in them—for what an exchange do they imply! John, in whom she was to behold all of us, could become her child only at the cost of Christ; a mere man must henceforth take the place, for the rest of her earthly life, of God Himself; and, whatever comfort St. John may be to her afterwards, the very thought of the contrast at the moment brings her terrible loss more vividly before her than anything else could have done. In short, the death-warrant of Mary's divine maternity seems to be conveyed in the very same words that bring to pass her human motherhood; and thus her heart is opened wide to admit us by a piercing sword indeed.

Holy Scripture as well as natural affection tells us "not to forget the groanings of our Mother".[1] Let no Christian who sees His mother Mary, when Jesus has given up the Ghost, standing desolate beneath the Cross for His sake, forget that she helped to bring Him forth to grace in pain and anguish; and let him further remember that the sharpest sting of all her sorrows lay in the fear that so many of the dearly-bought race would make her Son's death of no avail

[1] Ecclesiasticus vii. 29.

On the Blessed Virgin's Compassion.

by rejecting, of their own free will, the grace it won for them. Keeping this thought in mind, it will surely not be difficult, for any of us who may be crucifying Christ over again by mortal sin, to use this solemn time of His passion for " bringing forth fruits worthy of penance," and so consoling and rejoicing that torn and wounded Mother's Heart by our own loving tears of sorrow.

IX.

THE ASSUMPTION OF MARY.

" Quæ est ista quæ ascendit de deserto, deliciis affluens, innixa super dilectum suum ? " (Cant. viii. 5).

THE succession of the Blessed Virgin's Feasts that we have followed has shown how wonderfully the Mysteries of Christianity are linked one with another; and this one, which celebrates the final event of her earthly life, has a special connection with the Incarnation of the Eternal Word. For if Mary once received Jesus her Saviour, it is fitting that the Saviour should in His turn receive Mary. He disdained not to come down to her; and now He will take her up to Himself and make her share His glory. It is but natural, therefore, to find the Holy Maiden rising in triumph from her tomb amid pomp and splendour. She gave her Son His human life; and He, being God, and hence bound to repay munificently, gives her in return the glorious Life of immortality. Thus are these two mysteries—of the Incarnation and the Assumption—linked; and, that there may be still closer relation between them, we may well believe that the Angels take part in both :—that they rejoice to-day with Mary, and are delighted to behold so beautiful a completion of the mystery whose beginnings they first announced.

Heaven, as well as earth, has its gala days and triumphs, its functions and solemn entries ; or, rather, earth borrows these names for its own vain pomps. Magnificence can in fact only be realised to its fullest extent in the splendid festivals of the heavenly Jerusalem ; and of all the glorious solemnities that have rejoiced the holy angels and the spirits of the Blessed, we may be sure that the one we are keeping to-day is among the most illustrious. The raising of the Blessed Virgin to the throne prepared for her by her Son must indeed be the occasion of a most joyful day in Eternity :—if we may speak of *days* in the Everlasting City. To describe Mary's entry into Heaven I might try to bring before you the great concourse of its inhabitants, with the acclamations and glad canticles of the nine orders of Angels and the whole heavenly Court. I might even go higher, and show you the Mother of God presented by her Divine Son before the Father's throne, there to receive from His Hand her crown of immortal glory. But my object here is not so much to dwell on the *effects* of her Assumption, in her attainment of glory, as to consider what were its *causes ;* and for this purpose it will be better for us to think most, not of the heavenly court that receives her above but of the virtues that accompany her from below. These virtues, in fact, form her chief glory, since they both prepared her for the bliss she has attained and will themselves cause its fullest perfection throughout eternity.

That Mary might enter into her glory she had, first, to be stripped of this wretched mortality, as of a garment foreign to her; then, her body and soul had to be "clothed upon" with immortality, as with a royal mantle or triumphal robe; and lastly, clad in this superb apparel, she had to be placed on her throne, above the cherubim and seraphim and all other creatures. Now, it may be truly said that the whole of this great work was wrought by three special virtues which shone forth above all others in the Mother of Christ: namely, those of Divine Love, Holy Chastity, and Perfect Humility. I shall try to set forth the special relation of each of these virtues to the three steps of the Blessed Virgin's entry into Eternal Bliss.

I.

Nature and grace concur in establishing the unchangeable necessity of *dying*. It is a law of nature that everything mortal owes tribute to death; and grace has not exempted man from the hard necessity because the Son of God determined to destroy death by means of death itself. He has therefore laid down the law that we must pass through its very hands to escape from it, and go down into the tomb to rise again. In short, to strip mortality of its power we

The Assumption of Mary. 135

must all die. Therefore the sacred pageant of to-day had to be preceded by Mary's decease: she could not attain to her triumph without first submitting to the law of Death, and leaving behind in his clutches—so to speak—everything belonging to her that was mortal.

But, though the Blessed Virgin was subjected to this common law, it does not necessarily follow that she had to undergo it in the ordinary way. Death itself is, indeed, the lot of all; but its *principle* may vary in different cases. Now, everything in Mary's career was supernatural: she received Jesus Christ in the beginning miraculously, and it is but to be expected that she should have back her well-beloved Son, at the end, also by a miracle. Further, it seems a fitting completion to a life so full of marvels as was hers that the principle of her death should be not a human, but a divine, one. Hence, granting that some supernatural cause is to be looked for here, we have only to seek for the special one; and I hold it to be certain that Mary's human life came to an end simply through the working of *Divine Love*. The strength of this, hourly increasing in her throughout her mortal life, at last burst asunder the bonds of flesh and bore away her soul to be reunited with the Son from Whom she had been parted only by a violent wrench. Such a death is a sacred mystery; but we may to some extent realise how it might come to pass by yet once more calling to mind what has been so often dwelt upon in following the whole chain of events in the

Blessed Virgin's life:—namely, the *source* and *nature* of her love for Jesus. To draw this matter out again in full detail would be superfluous; but I may here quote, as specially applicable to our present subject, the words of a very holy man which beautifully summarise all that has gone before, and bring out with striking force the peculiar characteristics of Mary's maternal affection. Amadeus of Lausanne—a Bishop of the twelfth century—in a homily on the Blessed Virgin's praises, has the following passage: "To form Mary's love, two loves were united; for she gave to her Son the love due to a God, and to her God the love due to a Son".[1] This is a sublime way of saying that *Nature and Grace concurred* in making the deepest possible impression on Mary's heart, as there is nothing stronger or more efficacious than the love given by nature for a son, and that given by grace for God. These two loves are two abysses, whose depths we cannot sound and whose extent we cannot take in. But in face of them we may truly say, with the Psalmist: *Abyssus abyssum invocat:*[2] "deep calleth unto deep"—since, to form the Blessed Virgin's love, the tenderest feelings of nature and the most powerful forces of grace met together. Nature had to be present because the Love was for a son, and grace because it related to a God. Ordinary nature and ordinary grace would, of course, not have sufficed to create such an affection; but we know, from our

[1] *De Laudib. B. Virg.*, Homil. v. [2] Ps. xli. 8.

previous searchings into the origin of Mary's maternity, that both nature and grace in her were *extraordinary*. Hence a little reflection on the workings of this double love within her, after she had been left on earth without Him Who was its object, may give us some faint idea of how it might pierce and wound her heart with its longings till the frail body could bear it no longer :—and thus become, as I have said above, truly the cause of her death. It is held by Catholic tradition that the Mother of God remained some time on earth after Our Lord's ascension, it being His pleasure that she should stay to comfort and help the infant Church during the early days of His departure. If we would understand, in ever so faint a degree, what must have been her impatience to rejoin Him during all those years, we must try to measure it by her love. There can, I think, be no exaggeration in believing that, had God not *willed* her to live in this world for a certain time, any one of the sighs of longing that her heart breathed forth would have been strong enough to bear her soul away to its desired goal. Indeed, it would be almost truer to say that the Blessed Virgin's death, caused by Divine Love, was the *cessation* of a miracle than that it was itself miraculous ; for the real miracle lay rather in her being able to live on earth for so long parted from her Beloved.

Believing, then, that excess of love alone brought about the ending of this wondrous life, we may go on to ask in what particular way the death-blow was given? Did some more strongly-inflamed desire—some more violent transport—than any before, come to carry off Mary's soul? I venture to hold that it was not so; but that when the appointed time for her release had come it was wrought simply by the gradual perfecting of her love, which—having always reigned in her heart without the slightest obstacle—at last reached such perfection that an earthly body could no longer contain it. Then the holy Mother gave up her happy soul into the hands of her Son: not by any sudden or extraordinary special movement, but gently and sweetly. Even as the lightest touch will make a ripe fruit drop from its stem, so was this perfect spirit gathered in one moment to its heavenly home, without effort or shock—needing nought to carry it upwards save its own holy desires.

Thus did Mary's Love reunite her soul to Jesus through a happy death, which consigned her body to the tomb. But the mortal part of Christ's mother was not to stay long within the shadow of the grave; and we must now go on to see the effects of Holy Chastity in helping to bring it forth.

2.

Mary's sacred body—the throne of Chastity, the temple of Incarnate Wisdom, the instrument of the Holy Ghost, the seat of the Power of the Most High—could not remain in the tomb. Her triumph would be incomplete if it took place apart from her holy

The Assumption of Mary. 139

flesh; for this, expressly sanctified to form the body of Christ, had been as it were the source of all her glory. The Blessed Virgin's flesh, we know, was *virginal* flesh; and the power of holy virginity had worked three special wonders therein. It had saved it from corruption, drawn down heavenly influence upon it, and surrounded it with divine light. These three marvellous effects of virginity in her flesh had in their turn produced three conditions which, together, resulted in the assumption of her body from the tomb.

First, the fact that Mary's flesh was saved by the virtue of holy chastity from corruption prevented it from being dissolved, like that of mankind in general, at death. We have seen how, at the first moment of her existence, Mary's body and soul alike were preserved from the stain of concupiscence, so that they possessed perfect integrity. Now, to grasp fully the necessary effect of this miracle—which we call the "Immaculate Conception"—on her whole nature, it is absolutely necessary to understand clearly what this freedom from concupiscence, in her, meant. St. Thomas tells us we are not to suppose that the extraordinary grace bestowed upon Mary merely *tempered*—as in others among the elect—the fire of concupiscence. He says that not only were evil works, evil desires, and even wrong inclinations, destroyed in her; but that the very origin of the fire itself—the *first spark*, so to speak, whence the flame of concupiscence might spring—what theology calls *fomes peccati*—was utterly extinguished. Further, entirely to elucidate the point that I wish to make clear, I must ask you to remember what is Christian teaching as to the ordinary cause of death in our sinful race. We may not hold, with mere men of science, that it is simply a necessary consequence of the composite nature of our bodies. We are bound to raise our thoughts higher, and to believe that what subjects our flesh to the law of corruption is the fact that it attracts what is evil and is a source of bad desires: in short, as St. Paul says, that it is *caro peccati*.[1] Flesh such as this has to be destroyed, even in the elect; because whilst it remains "a flesh of sin," it is unworthy to be united to a glorious soul, or to enter into the Kingdom of God, which "flesh and blood cannot possess".[2] It must, then, change its original form that it may be renewed, and lose its first life to receive a second from the hand of its Maker. For God allows this flesh of ours, all disordered as it is by concupiscence, to fall into ruins, that He may rebuild it Himself according to His first plan at its creation. This is what we must hold as to bodily corruption if we would follow the teaching of the Gospels, from which we learn that our flesh has to be turned to dust because it has been the servant of sin; whence we cannot fail to see that Mary's flesh, being absolutely pure, must in consequence be incorruptible.

[1] Rom. viii. 3.   [2] Cor. xv. 50.

The Assumption of Mary. 141

And it was for the same reason—*i.e.*, through the action of its virginal purity—that her flesh was destined to be endowed prematurely with the gift of immortality. Though God has fixed upon some particular moment for the general resurrection of the dead, He may yet be compelled for special reasons to anticipate that time in favour of the Blessed Virgin. An apt illustration of such forestalling may be found in a common earthly phenomenon. The sun naturally brings forth fruit only in its due season; but there are certain modes of cultivation which cause plants to experience his influence more quickly, and to spring up and bear fruit long before that season arrives. Even so there are "forced" plants in the garden of our Heavenly Spouse; and Mary's holy flesh was a substance prepared for producing the fruits of immortality before the commonly appointed time, by the peculiar heavenly influence drawn down upon it through its perfect chastity. In fact, its *conformity with the Flesh of Christ* fitted it to receive a specially prompt effect from His quickening power. Our Lord had taken upon Him that virginal flesh—had dwelt enclosed within it for nine months—had *loved* it so much as actually to incorporate Himself with it. It is not, therefore, to be supposed that He would leave a body so well beloved as this in the tomb. He would naturally bear it away immediately to Heaven, clothed in immortal glory.

And this glory, again—this robe of Immortality—will be the effect of Mary's Immaculate Conception:

and for this reason:—Jesus Christ, in His Gospel, represents the glory of risen bodies to us by saying that we shall be in heaven "as the angels of God".[1] Hence Tertullian, speaking of risen flesh, calls it "angelicised flesh"—*angelificata caro*. Now, of all the Christian virtues, the one that chiefly forms angels on earth is Holy Chastity. St. Augustine has said of it that "whilst dwelling *in* the flesh it has a quality not *of* the flesh,"[2] and which partakes rather of the angel than of the man. A virtue that has power to produce angels even in this life may well produce them in the future one; and we have therefore good reason to believe that chastity plays a most special part in clothing our risen bodies with their glorious garments of immortality at the Last Day. If Mary's body, then, because of its conformity with the body of Our Saviour, surpasses the very Spirits of Heaven in purity, what may we not imagine its glory to be! To give us some slight notion of it, Holy Scripture has placed the moon under her feet and the stars above her head; whilst it has represented the sun as piercing her through and surrounding her with his rays:—*Mulier amicta Sole:*[3] this being the only image that earth could afford brilliant enough to symbolise the beauty and splendour that must clothe the Mother of God in her risen state.

---

[1] Matt. xxii. 30.

[2] "Habet aliquid jam non carnis in carne."—*De Sancta Virginit.* n. 12, tom. vi.

[3] Apoc. xii. 2.

The Assumption of Mary.

3.

Such, then, was the work of Virginal Purity in Mary's flesh. The only point now left to consider is what particular relation her perfert Humility of heart has to her final triumph. We shall understand this best by a further comparison of her with her Divine Son, for the triumph of Christ—His victory over sin and death—was brought about solely by Humility: by the humbleness of perfect obedience to His Father's Will. Now, Mary could not really rejoice in her triumph if she were to reach it by any other way than the one that her Son Himself had chosen; and hence we may be sure that by Humility only she was raised to her throne, and in the following manner:—

The property of true humility is to strip and impoverish itself, but at the same time to clothe and enrich itself in a marvellous way by its own very act, because whatever it gives up it assuredly gets back. It cannot be better described than by St. Paul's expression: "having nothing, yet possessing all things "[1]; and by shortly recalling the chief sacrifices of Mary's life we shall see how perfectly this description may be applied to her mode of practising the virtue.

The Blessed Virgin had three most perfect possessions. She had her high dignity; her wondrous purity of body and soul; and her motherhood of Jesus

[1] Coloss. i. 19.

Devotion to the Blessed Virgin.

Christ:—she had for her own Son Him in Whom St. Paul says "it hath well pleased the Father that all fulness should dwell". In her, then, we have a creature greatly distinguished beyond her kind; but we find that her deep humility strips her in a sense of all these wonderful privileges. Though raised far above others by her dignity as Mother of God, she lives a life of obscure service as one of the common herd; though separated from all by her immaculate purity she mixes in the society of sinners, and purifies herself as they do. But she does more than this: from Calvary she even loses her well-beloved Son. And she does not merely lose Him by seeing Him die a cruel death, but by His ceasing, in a certain sense, to be her Son at all and by His substituting another for Himself: "Woman," He says to her, "behold thy son!" Be sure that Our Saviour did not speak in this way to His Mother without reason. He would not appear not to know her—would not call her *Woman* instead of Mother—if there were no deep mystery hidden beneath His action; and the reason of it may be found in the state of abject humiliation in which Our Lord then was, and which He willed that His holy Mother should share with Him by the closest possible imitation. We must remember, here, that Jesus had a God for His Father, and Mary a God for her Son. At the moment we are speaking of, the Saviour had lost His Father, *as a father*, and called upon Him only as His God. Mary, then, must lose her Son, to correspond with this supreme sacrifice ; and hence He addresses her now as "woman," and not as "mother". Further, which is the deepest humiliation of all, He gives her another son ; as though henceforth He would cease to be hers, and meant to break the bond of their sacred union. St Paulinus gives as Christ's reason for this act that whereas, so long as He lived His mortal life on earth, He had paid every possible honour and service that a son could pay to His Mother, and had been her constant consolation and support, now that He was on the eve of entering into His glory He assumed an attitude more suited to the dignity of God ; and therefore gave up the natural duties of filial love to another. Thus was Mary left with St. John for her son in the place of Jesus, Who had Himself instituted the exchange. She humbly accepted the humiliating decree, and took the disciple instead of the Master—the son of Zebedee instead of the Son of God (as St. Bernard says)—to her maternal heart ; and so she lived for many years on earth, only thinking in her humility that she deserved not to be the Mother of God.

But if Mary was thus perfectly stripped of everything, that her humiliation in this world might bear a close likeness to her Divine Son's, she was to have all back in full, and more than full, measure ; her humility was not only to "have nothing," but to "possess all things". Because she made herself the servant of others she is to be raised to a throne ;

because she purified herself—being all pure — as though a sinner, she is to be the advocate of sinners, and their refuge next after Christ: *Refugium peccatorum;* and because she gave up her Son, and patiently and humbly bore His apparent desertion of her, that beloved Son will now enter once more into His filial rights—which He had ceded to John but for a time —and will present her before the whole heavenly court as His Mother.

Thus, then, are the words of my text fully verified in Mary's glorious Assumption. Truly, indeed, may we say that she "cometh up from the desert, flowing with delights, leaning on her Beloved"; for the arm of her Divine Son supports her, His well-known voice makes music in her ear, and her heart overflows with heavenly joy at the thought that it is to *His* merits and love alone that she owes every gift that she has received, and all the songs of praise wherewith the Angelic Hosts greet the entrance of their Queen. Surely we may without presumption imagine the Patriarchs and Prophets of the old Law echoing, as it were, the last words of her own magnificent canticle, when they see the mother of the Messias Whom they had prophesied appear, by uttering some of their own inspired sayings. Moses would surely cry as he beheld Mary assume her throne, " A star shall rise out of Jacob and a sceptre shall spring up from Israel ";[1] Isaias, seized with the spirit of God, would

[1] Num. xxiv. 17.

sing in a rapture of delight: "Here is that Virgin who was to conceive and bear a Son";[1] Ezekiel would recognise in the Virgin Mother that "shut gate"[2] that was never again to be opened because "the Lord the God of Israel hath entered in by it"; whilst Royal David, standing in the midst, would intone, to a heavenly lyre, his grand song: "On Thy right hand stood the Queen in golden raiment, wrought about with variety. All the glory of the King's daughter is from within, in fringes of gold, wrought with divers colours. After her shall virgins be brought unto the King—her neighbours shall be brought unto Thee. With joy and gladness shall they be brought unto the King."[3]

Mary, meantime, will once more pour forth her *Magnificat* and sing the praises of God, Who by all this honour bestowed upon her has indeed gloriously rewarded *the humility of His Handmaid.*

[1] Isaiah vii. 14.   [2] Ezek. xliv. 2.
[3] Ps. xliv., 10, 14, 15, 16.

Note to Sermon II.,
ON MARY'S CONCEPTION.

It may be a help to the full understanding and enjoyment of this sermon to remind readers of three things :—*i.e.*

(1) That it was preached whilst the Truth of the Blessed Virgin's Immaculate Conception, though almost universally held by the Faithful, was still in the stage of being *under consideration* as a matter *for definition*: hence Bossuet's care to speak of it undogmatically.

(2) That the teaching of the Catholic Church with regard to original sin is as follows, according to the decrees of the Council of Trent :—that 'Adam, when in Paradise he disobeyed 'the command of God, at once lost the sanctity and justice in 'which he had been instituted, and incurred by this transgres-'sion the anger and wrath of God; and also the punishment of 'death with which God had threatened him ; and, with death, 'captivity under the power of him who "had the empire of 'death, that is to say, the devil"; and that by that transgression 'Adam, both in his soul and body, was changed for the worse.

'Nor let any one say that Adam injured himself alone and 'not his progeny, and that he lost the sanctity and justice he 'had received from God for himself alone, and not for us also. 'Nor that he, thus stained by the sin of disobedience, trans-'fused into the whole human race death and bodily suffering, 'but not sin; for then he would contradict the words of the 'Apostle "by one man sin entered into this world, and by sin 'death, and so death passed upon all men in whom all have 'sinned" (Rom. v. 12).

'Nor can any one say that this sin of Adam which is one 'in origin and by propagation, not by imitation, transferred to 'all, can be taken away by any other remedy than by the merit 'of this one Mediator our Lord Jesus Christ, who has reconciled 'us to God by His blood—and that merit of Jesus Christ is 'applied both to infants and adults by the sacrament of 'baptism.'

(3) That what the Church means by the "Immaculate Conception" of the mother of God is that at the moment of her *passive*[1] conception—that is, at the very first instant when her *soul was infused into her body*—she was sanctified by God's grace; so that her soul was never deprived of that sanctification which the rest of mankind had forfeited by the sin of Adam. It never from its first creation was displeasing to God. It was never stained by original sin.

It cannot be better expressed than by the definition given in the Encyclical of Pope Pius IX. on the 8th of December, 1854:—

"Being full of confidence in God, and persuaded that the fitting moment was come for defining the Immaculate Conception of the most holy Virgin Mother of God, which is attested and wonderfully illustrated by the Divine Oracles, venerable tradition, the permanent feeling of the Church, the admirable agreement of Catholic pastors and their flocks, and the solemn acts of our predecessors; after having examined everything with the greatest care, and offered assiduous and fervent prayers to God, it has seemed to us that we ought no longer to delay to sanction and define by our supreme judgment the Immaculate Conception of the Virgin, and thus to satisfy the pious desires of the Catholic world and our own devotion towards the most holy Virgin, in order to honour

---

[1] For the distinction between "active" and "passive" Conception, see *The Immaculate Conception* by Bishop Ullathorne, chap. vi.; also Father Harper's *Peace through the Truth*.

more and more, in her, her only Son our Lord Jesus Christ, since all the praise and honour which we give to the Mother redounds to the glory of the Son. Therefore . . . we declare, pronounce, and define that the doctrine according to which the Blessed Virgin Mary was, from the first moment of her Conception, by a singular grace and special privilege of Almighty God, for the sake of the merits of Jesus Christ, the Saviour of Mankind, preserved and exempted from all stain of original sin, is revealed by God, and consequently should be firmly and constantly believed by all the faithful. If, then, any one —which God forbid—has the presumption to think in his heart otherwise than we have defined, let him learn and know that being condemned by his own judgment, he has made shipwreck of the faith and forsaken the Church.'

OF
THEOLOGICAL BOOKS
(MAINLY ROMAN CATHOLIC)
PUBLISHED BY
LONGMANS, GREEN, & CO.
LONDON, NEW YORK, AND BOMBAY.

MESSRS. LONGMANS, GREEN, & CO.

Issue the undermentioned Catalogues and Lists of their Publications, any of which may be had post free on application:—

1. MONTHLY LIST OF NEW BOOKS AND NEW EDITIONS.
2. QUARTERLY LIST OF ANNOUNCEMENTS AND NEW BOOKS.
3. NOTES ON BOOKS: BEING AN ANALYSIS OF THE WORKS PUBLISHED BY MESSRS. LONGMANS, GREEN & CO. DURING EACH QUARTER.
4. SCIENTIFIC AND TECHNICAL BOOKS.
5. MEDICAL AND SURGICAL BOOKS.
6. EDUCATIONAL AND SCHOOL BOOKS.
7. EDUCATIONAL BOOKS RECENTLY PUBLISHED.
8. BOOKS FOR ELEMENTARY SCHOOLS AND PUPIL TEACHERS.
9. BOOKS FOR SCHOOL PRIZES
10. BOOKS FOR CHRISTMAS AND NEW YEAR PRESENTS.
11. THEOLOGICAL BOOKS (CHURCH OF ENGLAND).
12. THEOLOGICAL BOOKS (MAINLY ROMAN CATHOLIC).
13. BOOKS IN GENERAL LITERATURE AND GENERAL THEOLOGY.
14. A CLASSIFIED CATALOGUE (144 pp.) (GENERAL LITERATURE, SCIENCE, THEOLOGY, EDUCATION).

CARDINAL NEWMAN'S WORKS.

Letters and Correspondence of John Henry Newman during his Life in the English Church. With a brief Autobiography. Edited, at Cardinal Newman's request, by ANNE MOZLEY. 2 vols. Cr. 8vo. 7s.

Parochial and Plain Sermons. Edited by REV. W. J. COPELAND, B.D. late Rector of Farnham, Essex. 8 vols. Sold separately. Crown 8vo. Cabinet Edition, 5s. each; Popular Edition, 3s. 6d. each.

CONTENTS OF VOL. I.:—Holiness necessary for Future Blessedness—The Immortality of the Soul—Knowledge of God's Will without Obedience—Secret Faults—Self-Denial the Test of Religious Earnestness—The Spiritual Mind—Sins of Ignorance and Weakness—God's Commandments not Grievous—The Religious Use of Excited Feelings—Profession without Practice—Profession without Hypocrisy—Profession without Ostentation—Promising without Doing—Religious Emotion—Religious Faith Rational—The Christian Mysteries—The Self-Wise Inquirer—Obedience the Remedy for Religious Perplexity—Times of Private Prayer—Forms of Private Prayer—The Resurrection of the Body—Witnesses of the Resurrection—Christian Reverence—The Religion of the Day—Scripture a Record of Human Sorrow—Christian Manhood.

CONTENTS OF VOL. II.:—The World's Benefactors—Faith without Sight—The Incarnation—Martyrdom—Love of Relations and Friends—The Mind of Little Children—Ceremonies of the Church—The Glory of the Christian Church—St. Paul's Conversion viewed in Reference to his Office—Secrecy and Suddenness of Divine Visitations—Divine Decrees—The Reverence Due to the Blessed Virgin Mary—Christ, a Quickening Spirit—Saving Knowledge—Self-Contemplation—Religious Cowardice—The Gospel Witnesses—Mysteries in Religion—The Indwelling Spirit—The Kingdom of the Saints—The Gospel, a Trust Committed to us—Tolerance of Religious Error—Rebuking Sin—The Christian Ministry—Human Responsibility—Guilelessness—The Danger of Riches—The Powers of Nature—The Danger of Accomplishments—Christian Zeal—Use of Saints' Days.

CARDINAL NEWMAN'S WORKS.

Parochial and Plain Sermons.—*Continued.*

CONTENTS OF VOL. III.:—Abraham and Lot—Wilfulness of Israel in Rejecting Samuel—Saul—Early Years of David—Jeroboam—Faith and Obedience—Christian Repentance—Contracted Views in Religion—A Particular Providence as revealed in the Gospel—Tears of Christ at the Grave of Lazarus—Bodily Suffering—The Humiliation of the Eternal Son—Jewish Zeal a Pattern to Christians—Submission to Church Authority—Contest between Truth and Falsehood in the Church—The Church Visible and Invisible—The Visible Church an Encouragement to Faith—The Gift of the Spirit—Regenerating Baptism—Infant Baptism—The Daily Service—The Good Part of Mary—Religious Worship a Remedy for Excitements—Intercession—The Intermediate State.

CONTENTS OF VOL IV.:—The Strictness of the Law of Christ—Obedience without Love, as instanced in the Character of Balaam—Moral Consequences of Single Sins—Acceptance of Religious Privileges Compulsory—Reliance on Religious Observances—The Individuality of the Soul—Chastisement amid Mercy—Peace and Joy amid Chastisement—The State of Grace—The Visible Church for the Sake of the Elect—The Communion of Saints—The Church a Home for the Lonely—The Invisible World—The Greatness and Littleness of Human Life—Moral Effects of Communion with God—Christ Hidden from the World—Christ Manifested in Remembrance—The Gainsaying of Korah—The Mysteriousness of our Present Being—The Ventures of Faith—Faith and Love—Watching—Keeping Fast and Festival.

CONTENTS OF VOL. V.:—Worship, a Preparation for Christ's Coming—Reverence, a Belief in God's Presence—Unreal Words—Shrinking from Christ's Coming—Equanimity—Remembrance of Past Mercies—The Mystery of Godliness—The State of Innocence—Christian Sympathy—Righteousness not of us, but in us—The Law of the Spirit—The New Works of the Gospel—The State of Salvation—Transgressions and Infirmities—Sins of Infirmity—Sincerity and Hypocrisy—The Testimony of Conscience—Many called, Few chosen—Present Blessings—Endurance, the Christian's Portion—Affliction, a School of Comfort—The Thought of God, the Stay of the Soul—Love, the One Thing Needful—The Power of the Will.

CONTENTS OF VOL. VI.:—Fasting, a Source of Trial—Life, the Season of Repentance—Apostolic Abstinence, a Pattern for Christians—Christ's Privations, a Meditation for Christians—Christ the Son of God made Man—The Incarnate Son, a Sufferer and Sacrifice—The Cross of Christ the Measure of the World—Difficulty of realising Sacred Privileges—The Gospel Sign Addressed to Faith—The Spiritual Presence of Christ in the Church—The Eucharistic Presence—Faith the Title for Justification—Judaism of the Present Day—The Fellowship of the Apostles—Rising with Christ—Warfare the Condition of Victory—Waiting for Christ—Subjection of the Reason and Feelings to the Revealed Word—The Gospel Palaces—The Visible Temple—Offerings for the Sanctuary—The Weapons of Saints—Faith Without Demonstration—The Mystery of the Holy Trinity—Peace in Believing.

CONTENTS OF VOL. VII.:—The Lapse of Time—Religion, a Weariness to the Natural Man—The World our Enemy—The Praise of Men—Temporal Advantages—The Season of Epiphany—The Duty of Self-Denial—The Yoke of Christ—Moses the Type of Christ—The Crucifixion—Attendance on Holy Communion—The Gospel Feast—Love of Religion, a new Nature—Religion Pleasant to the Religious—Mental Prayer—Infant Baptism—The Unity of the Church—Steadfastness in the Old Paths.

CONTENTS OF VOL. VIII.:—Reverence in Worship—Divine Calls—The Trial of Saul—The Call of David—Curiosity, a Temptation to Sin—Miracles no Remedy for Unbelief—Josiah, a Pattern for the Ignorant—Inward Witness to the Truth of the Gospel—Jeremiah, a Lesson for the Disappointed—Endurance of the World's Censure—Doing Glory to God in Pursuits of the World—Vanity of Human Glory—Truth Hidden when not Sought after—Obedience to God the Way to Faith in Christ—Sudden Conversions—The Shepherd of our Souls—Religious Joy—Ignorance of Evil.

Sermons Preached on Various Occasions. Crown 8vo. Cabine Edition, 6s.; Popular Edition, 3s. 6d.

CONTENTS:—Intellect the Instrument of Religious Training—The Religion of the Pharisee and the Religion of Mankind—Waiting for Christ—The Secret Power of Divine Grace—Dispositions for Faith—Omnipotence in Bonds—St. Paul's Characteristic Gift—St. Paul's Gift of Sympathy—Christ upon the Waters—The Second Spring—Order, the Witness and Instrument of Unity—The Mission of St. Philip Neri—The Tree beside the Waters—In the World but not of the World—The Pope and the Revolution.

CARDINAL NEWMAN'S WORKS.

Selection, Adapted to the Seasons of the Ecclesiastical Year, from the 'Parochial and Plain Sermons'. Edited by the REV. W. J. COPELAND, B.D. Crown 8vo. Cabinet Edition, 5s.; Popular Edition, 3s. 6d.

CONTENTS:—*Advent*: Self-Denial the Test of Religious Earnestness—Divine Calls—The Ventures of Faith—Watching. *Christmas Day*: Religious Joy. *New Year's Sunday*: The Lapse of Time. *Epiphany*: Remembrance of Past Mercies — Equanimity—The Immortality of the Soul — Christian Manhood — Sincerity and Hypocrisy — Christian Sympathy. *Septuagesima*: Present Blessings. *Sexagesima*: Endurance, the Christian's Portion. *Quinquagesima*: Love, the One Thing Needful. *Lent*: The Individuality of the Soul—Life, the Season of Repentance—Bodily Suffering—Tears of Christ at the Grave of Lazarus—Christ's Privations, a Meditation for Christians—The Cross of Christ the Measure of the World. *Good Friday*: The Crucifixion. *Easter Day*: Keeping Fast and Festval. *Easter Tide*: Witnesses of the Resurrection—A Particular Providence as revealed in the Gospel—Christ Manifested in Remembrance—The Invisible World—Waiting for Christ. *Ascension*: Warfare the Condition of Victory. *Sunday after Ascension*: Rising with Christ. *Whitsun Day*: The Weapons of Saints. *Trinity Sunday*: The Mysteriousness of our Present Being. *Sundays after Trinity*: Holiness Necessary for Future Blessedness—The Religious Use of Excited Feelings—The Self-Wise Inquirer—Scripture a Record of Human Sorrow—The Danger of Riches—Obedience without Love, as instanced in the Character of Balaam—Moral Consequences of Single Sins—The Greatness and Littleness of Human Life—Moral Effects of Communion with God—The Thought of God the Stay of the Soul—The Power of the Will—The Gospel Palaces—Religion a Weariness to the Natural Man—The World our Enemy—The Praise of Men—Religion Pleasant to the Religious—Mental Prayer—Curiosity a Temptation to Sin—Miracles no Remedy for Unbelief—Jeremiah, a Lesson for the Disappointed—The Shepherd of our Souls—Doing Glory to God in Pursuits of the World.

Sermons Bearing upon Subjects of the Day. Edited by the REV. W. J. COPELAND, B.D., late Rector of Farnham, Essex. Crown 8vo. Cabinet Edition, 5s.; Popular Edition, 3s. 6d.

CONTENTS:—The Work of the Christian—Saintliness not Forfeited by the Penitent—Our Lord's Last Supper and His First—Dangers to the Penitent—The Three Offices of Christ—Faith and Experience—Faith unto the World—The Church and the World—Indulgence in Religious Privileges—Connection between Personal and Public Improvement—Christian Nobleness—Joshua a Type of Christ and His Followers—Elisha a Type of Christ and His Followers—The Christian Church a Continuation of the Jewish—The Principles of Continuity between the Jewish and Christian Churches—The Christian Church an Imperial Power—Sanctity the Token of the Christian Empire—Condition of the Members of the Christian Empire—The Apostolic Christian—Wisdom and Innocence—Invisible Presence of Christ—Outward and Inward Notes of the Church—Grounds for Steadfastness in our Religious Profession—Elijah the Prophet of the Latter Days—Feasting in Captivity—The Parting of Friends.

Fifteen Sermons Preached before the University of Oxford, between A.D. 1826 and 1843. Crown 8vo. Cabinet Edition, 5s.; Popular Edition, 3s. 6d.

CONTENTS:—The Philosophical Temper, first enjoined by the Gospel—The Influence of Natural and Revealed Religion respectively—Evangelical Sanctity the Perfection of Natural Virtue—The Usurpations of Reason—Personal Influence, the Means of Propagating the Truth—On Justice as a Principle of Divine Governance—Contest between Faith and Sight—Human Responsibility, as independent of Circumstances—Wilfulness, the Sin of Saul—Faith and Reason, contrasted as Habits of Mind—The Nature of Faith in Relation to Reason—Love, the Safeguard of Faith against Superstition—Implicit and Explicit Reason—Wisdom, as contrasted with Faith and with Bigotry—The Theory of Developments in Religious Doctrine.

CARDINAL NEWMAN'S WORKS.

Apologia pro Vita Sua. Crown 8vo. Cabinet Edition, 6s.; Popular Edition, 3s. 6d.

Verses on Various Occasions. Crown 8vo. Cabinet Edition, 6s.; Popular Edition, 3s. 6d.

Discourses Addressed to Mixed Congregations. Crown 8vo. Cabinet Edition, 6s.; Popular Edition, 3s. 6d.

CONTENTS:—The Salvation of the Hearer the Motive of the Preacher—Neglect of Divine Calls and Warnings—Men not Angels—The Priests of the Gospel—Purity and Love—Saintliness the Standard of Christian Principle—God's Will the End of Life—Perseverance in Grace—Nature and Grace—Illuminating Grace—Faith and Private Judgment—Faith and Doubt—Prospects of the Catholic Missioner—Mysteries of Nature and of Grace—The Mystery of Divine Condescension—The Infinitude of Divine Attributes—Mental Sufferings of our Lord in His Passion—The Glories of Mary for the Sake of Her Son—On the Fitness of the Glories of Mary.

Lectures on the Doctrine of Justification. Crown 8vo. Cabinet Edition, 5s.; Popular Edition, 3s. 6d.

CONTENTS:—Faith considered as the Instrumental Cause of Justification—Love considered as the Formal Cause of Justification—Primary Sense of the term 'Justification'—Secondary Senses of the term 'Justification'—Misuse of the term 'Just' or 'Righteous'—The Gift of Righteousness—The Characteristics of the Gift of Righteousness—Righteousness viewed as a Gift and as a Quality—Righteousness the Fruit of our Lord's Resurrection—The Office of Justifying Faith—The Nature of Justifying Faith—Faith viewed relatively to Rites and Works—On Preaching the Gospel—Appendix.

On the Development of Christian Doctrine. Crown 8vo. Cabinet Edition, 6s.; Popular Edition, 3s. 6d.

On the Idea of a University. Crown 8vo. Cabinet Edition, 7s.; Popular Edition, 3s. 6d.

An Essay in Aid of a Grammar of Assent. Crown 8vo. Cabinet Edition, 7s. 6d.; Popular Edition, 3s. 6d.

Two Essays on Miracles. 1. Of Scripture. 2. Of Ecclesiastical History. Crown 8vo. Cabinet Edition, 6s.; Popular Edition, 3s. 6d.

Discussions and Arguments. Crown 8vo. Cabinet Edition, 6s.; Popular Edition, 3s. 6d.

1. How to accomplish it. 2. The Antichrist of the Fathers. 3. Scripture and the Creed. 4. Tamworth Reading-room. 5. Who's to Blame? 6. An Argument for Christianity.

Essays, Critical and Historical. 2 vols. Crown 8vo. Cabinet Edition, 12s.; Popular Edition, 7s.

1. Poetry. 2. Rationalism. 3. Apostolic Tradition. 4. De la Mennais. 5. Palmer on Faith and Unity. 6. St. Ignatius. 7. Prospects of the Anglican Church. 8. The Anglo-American Church. 9. Countess of Huntingdon. 10. Catholicity of the Anglican Church. 11. The Antichrist of Protestants. 12. Milman's Christianity. 13. Reformation of the XI. Century. 14. Private Judgment. 15. Davison. 16. Keble.

CARDINAL NEWMAN'S WORKS.

Historical Sketches. 3 vols. Crown 8vo. Cabinet Edition, 6s. each; Popular Edition, 3s. 6d.

1. The Turks. 2. Cicero. 3. Apollonius. 4. Primitive Christianity. 5. Church of the Fathers. 6. St. Chrysostom. 7. Theodoret. 8. St. Benedict. 9. Benedictine Schools. 10. Universities. 11. Northmen and Normans. 12. Mediæval Oxford. 13. Convocation of Canterbury.

The Arians of the Fourth Century. Crown 8vo. Cabinet Edition, 6s.; Popular Edition, 3s. 6d.

Select Treatises of St. Athanasius in Controversy with the Arians. Freely translated. 2 vols. Crown 8vo. Cabinet Edition, 15s.; Popular Edition, 7s.

Theological Tracts. Crown 8vo. Cabinet Edition, 8s.; Popular Edition, 3s. 6d.

1. Dissertatiunculæ. 2. On the Text of the Seven Epistles of St. Ignatius. 3. Doctrinal Causes of Arianism. 4. Apollinarianism. 5. St. Cyril's Formula. 6. Ordo de Tempore. 7. Douay Version of Scriptures.

The Via Media of the Anglican Church. 2 Vols. Crown 8vo. Cabinet Edition, 6s. each; Popular Edition, 3s. 6d. each.

Vol. I. Prophetical Office of the Church.
Vol. II. Occasional Letters and Tracts.

Certain Difficulties felt by Anglicans in Catholic Teaching Considered. 2 vols.

Vol. I. Twelve Lectures. Crown 8vo. Cabinet Edition, 7s. 6d.; Popular Edition, 3s. 6d.
Vol. II. Letters to Dr. Pusey concerning the Blessed Virgin, and to the Duke of Norfolk in defence of the Pope and Council. Crown 8vo. Cabinet Edition, 5s. 6d.; Popular Edition. 3s. 6d.

Present Position of Catholics in England. Crown 8vo. Cabinet Edition, 7s. 6d.; Popular Edition, 3s. 6d.

Loss and Gain. The Story of a Convert. Crown 8vo. Cabinet Edition, 6s.; Popular Edition, 3s. 6d.

Callista. A Tale of the Third Century. Crown 8vo. Cabinet Edition, 6s.; Popular Edition, 3s. 6d.

The Dream of Gerontius. 16mo, sewed, 6d.; cloth, 1s.

Meditations and Devotions. Part I. Meditations for the Month of May. Novena of St. Philip. Part II. The Stations of the Cross. Meditations and Intercessions for Good Friday. Litanies, etc. Part III. Meditations on Christian Doctrine. Conclusion. Oblong Crown 8vo. 5s. *net.*

CARDINAL NEWMAN'S WORKS.
COMPLETION OF THE POPULAR EDITION.

Parochial and Plain Sermons. 8 vols. Each	3s. 6d.
Sermons preached on Various Occasions	3s. 6d.
Selection, from the Parochial and Plain Sermons	3s. 6d.
Sermons bearing on Subjects of the Day	3s. 6d.
Sermons preached before the University of Oxford	3s. 6d.
Discourses addressed to Mixed Congregations	3s. 6d.
Lectures on the Doctrine of Justification	3s. 6d.
On the Development of Christian Doctrine	3s. 6d.
On the Idea of a University	3s. 6d.
An Essay in Aid of a Grammar of Assent	3s. 6d.
Biblical and Ecclesiastical Miracles	3s. 6d.
Discussions and Arguments on Various Subjects	3s. 6d.
Essays, Critical and Historical. 2 vols.	7s. 0d.
Historical Sketches. 3 vols. Each	3s. 6d.
The Arians of the Fourth Century	3s. 6d.
The Via Media of the Anglican Church. 2 vols. Each	3s. 6d.
Difficulties felt by Anglicans considered. 2 vols. Each	3s. 6d.
Present Position of Catholics in England	3s. 6d.
Apologia pro Vita Sua	3s. 6d.
Theological Tracts	3s. 6d.
Select Treatises of St. Athanasius. 2 vols.	7s. 0d.
Verses on Various Occasions	3s. 6d.
Loss and Gain	3s. 6d.
Callista	3s. 6d.

BATIFFOL.—History of the Roman Breviary. By PIERRE BATIFFOL, Litt.D. Translated by ATWELL M. Y. BAYLAY, M.A., Vicar of Thurgarton, Notts. With a New Preface by the Author. Crown 8vo. 7s. 6d.

DOBRÉE.—Stories on the Rosary. By LOUISA EMILY DOBRÉE, Author of "Stories of the Seven Sacraments". Part I. Crown 8vo. 1s. 6d.

FOUARD.—The Christ, The Son of God. A Life of Our Lord and Saviour Jesus Christ. By the ABBÉ CONSTANT FOUARD, Honorary Cathedral Canon, Professor of the Faculty of Theology at Rouen, etc., etc. Translated from the Fifth Edition with the Author's sanction. By GEORGE F. X. GRIFFITH. With an Introduction by CARDINAL MANNING. Third Edition. With 3 Maps. 2 vols. Crown 8vo. 14s.

Saint Peter and the First Years of Christianity. By the ABBÉ CONSTANT FOUARD. Translated by GEORGE F. X. GRIFFITH. Crown 8vo. 9s.

St. Paul and His Missions. By the ABBÉ CONSTANT FOUARD. Translated, with the Author's sanction and co-operation, by GEORGE F. X. GRIFFITH. With 2 Maps. Crown 8vo. 9s.

CHRISTIAN BIOGRAPHIES:

Henri Dominique Lacordaire. A Biographical Sketch. By H. L. SIDNEY LEAR. With Frontispiece. Crown 8vo. 3s. 6d.

A Christian Painter of the Nineteenth Century; being the Life of Hippolyte Flandrin. By H. L. SIDNEY LEAR. Crown 8vo. 3s. 6d.

Bossuet and his Contemporaries. By H. L. SIDNEY LEAR. Crown 8vo. 3s. 6d.

Fénelon, Archbishop of Cambrai. A Biographical Sketch. By H. L. SIDNEY LEAR. Crown 8vo. 3s. 6d.

A Dominican Artist. A Sketch of the Life of the Rev. Père Besson, of the Order of St. Dominic. By H. L. SIDNEY LEAR. Crown 8vo. 3s. 6d.

The Life of Madame Louise de France, Daughter of Louis XV., also known as the Mother Thérèse de S. Augustin. By H. L. SIDNEY LEAR. Crown 8vo. 3s. 6d.

The Revival of Priestly Life in the Seventeenth Century in France. Charles de Condren—S. Philip Neri and Cardinal de Berulle—S. Vincent de Paul—S. Sulpice and Jean Jacques Olier. By H. L. SIDNEY LEAR. Crown 8vo. 3s. 6d.

Life of S. Francis de Sales, Bishop and Prince of Geneva. By H. L. SIDNEY LEAR. Crown 8vo. 3s. 6d.

Henri Perreyve. By A. GRATRY, PRÊTRE DE L'ORATOIRE, Professeur de Morale Évangélique à la Sorbonne, et Membre de l'Académie Française. Translated, by special permission, by H. L. SIDNEY LEAR. With Portrait. Crown 8vo. 3s. 6d.

DRANE—A Memoir of Mother Francis Raphael O.S.D. (Augusta Theodosia Drane), some time Prioress Provincial of the Congregation of Dominican Sisters of S. Catherine of Siena, Stone. With some of her Spiritual Notes and Letters. Edited by Rev. Father BERTRAND WILBERFORCE, O.P. With Portrait. Crown 8vo. 7s. 6d.

The History of St. Dominic, Founder of the Friar Preachers. By AUGUSTA THEODOSIA DRANE, author of "The History of St. Catherine of Siena and her Companions". With 32 Illustrations. 8vo. 15s.

FÉNELON.—Spiritual Letters to Men. By ARCHBISHOP FÉNELON. Translated by H. L. SIDNEY LEAR, author of "Life of Fénelon," "Life of S. Francis de Sales," etc., etc. 16mo. 2s. 6d.

Spiritual Letters to Women. By ARCHBISHOP FÉNELON. Translated by H. L. SIDNEY LEAR, author of "Life of Fénelon," "Life of S. Francis de Sales," etc., etc. 16mo. 2s. 6d.

GIBSON.—The Abbé de Lamennais and the Liberal Catholic Movement in France. By the Hon. W. GIBSON. With Portrait. 8vo. 12s. 6d.

A SELECT LIST OF WORKS.

JAMESON—Works by Mrs. Jameson:

Sacred and Legendary Art. With 19 Etchings and 197 Woodcuts. 2 vols. Cloth, gilt top. 20s. *net.*

Legends of the Madonna: The Virgin Mary as Represented in Sacred and Legendary Art. With 27 Etchings and 165 Woodcuts. 1 vol. Cloth, gilt top. 10s. *net.*

Legends of the Monastic Orders. With 11 Etchings and 88 Woodcuts. 1 vol. Cloth, gilt top. 10s. *net.*

History of the Saviour, His Types and Precursors. Completed by Lady Eastlake. With 13 Etchings and 281 Woodcuts. 2 vols. Cloth, gilt top. 20s. *net.*

LYONS.—Christianity or Infallibility—Both or Neither. By the Rev. Daniel Lyons. Crown 8vo. 5s.

RIVINGTON.—The Primitive Church and the See of Peter. By the Rev. Luke Rivington, D.D. With an Introduction by the Cardinal Archbishop of Westminster. 8vo. 16s.

TYRRELL.—Works by George Tyrrell, S.J.:

Nova et Vetera: Informal Meditations for Times of Spiritual Dryness. Crown 8vo. 6s.

Hard Sayings: a Selection of Meditations and Studies. Crown 8vo. 6s.

WISEMAN.—The Life and Times of Cardinal Wiseman. By Wilfrid Ward, Author of " William George Ward and the Catholic Revival ". With 3 Portraits. 2 vols. Crown 8vo. 24s.

MANUALS OF CATHOLIC PHILOSOPHY.

(*Stonyhurst Series.*)

Edited by RICHARD F. CLARKE, S.J.

Logic. By Richard F. Clarke, S.J., D.D. Crown 8vo. 5s.

First Principles of Knowledge. By John Rickaby, S.J. Crown 8vo. 5s.

Moral Philosophy (Ethics and Natural Law). By Joseph Rickaby, S.J. Crown 8vo. 5s.

General Metaphysics. By John Rickaby, S.J. Crown 8vo. 5s.

Psychology. By Michael Maher, S.J. Crown 8vo. 6s. 6d.

Natural Theology. By Bernard Boedder, S.J. Crown 8vo. 6s. 6d.

Political Economy. By Charles S. Devas. Crown 8vo. 6s. 6d.

ENGLISH MANUALS OF CATHOLIC THEOLOGY.

Outlines of Dogmatic Theology. By Sylvester Joseph Hunter, of the Society of Jesus. Crown 8vo. 3 vols., 6s. 6d. each.

LONDON, NEW YORK, AND BOMBAY:
LONGMANS, GREEN, & CO

www.ingramcontent.com/pod-product-compliance
Lightning Source LLC
Chambersburg PA
CBHW020257170426
43202CB00008B/405